Werkstücke

Atelier Bettina Kraus

including contributions from

Michael Beutler
Eva Grubinger
Bettina Kraus
Alicja Kwade
Isa Melsheimer
Nandini Oehlmann
Mathias Peppler

jovis

CONTENT

PROLOGUE

Bettina Kraus

The first sentence of the book is difficult to bring to paper, and takes me much longer than those that follow. In creative fields, it is generally much more difficult to begin with intellect than intuition. What do the beginnings of the work process look like in a discipline for which you are untrained? How does one get accustomed to an unfamiliar skill, to overcome those initial difficulties? In my case, the task is writing this prologue; for the many authors of this publication, it refers to the search for and invention of their first house.

Presented in this publication are the results of a two-year studio course with architecture debutantes, whose lack of trade knowledge and vibrant naivety were channeled to form the basis for a reflective design process. The aim was to encourage the participants to discover their personal fetishes and develop a distinguishable signature while searching for a method where not only does one's head not impede the hand, but also where ideas are not simply blindly followed and materialized.

For an experienced architect, an empty sheet of paper presents an exciting moment full of prospects. For an inexperienced architect, it often provides too many possible outcomes and a sense of paralysis. The gap between the suggestive sketch and the material model is a vast one. In order to narrow the transition between the second and third dimensions, our teaching begins with the production of an individual, handmade *Werkstück* intended to record each personal signature.

In trade and industry a *Werkstück*—or "workpiece"—is a distinct object made of solid material and worked on in some form or another; its production method is of little significance. It is the link between the finished *Werk*, or the desired outcome, and the *Stück* used to achieve the final result. With regard to the design process in our studio—and in contrast to a classic workpiece—the way such an object is formed is of great significance. During the confrontation with—or handling of—isolated architectural parameters such as the reconciliation of the interior space with the exterior appearance, functional causalities, or the selection of a suitable construction, the workpiece is gradually transformed into a building.

An essential prerequisite for spatializing a notion of life is the ability to recall internalized images based on past situational experiences. Accordingly it is necessary to practice, thereby actively enhancing the perceptive senses on various levels and allowing the eye to travel. This entails simultaneously looking back at personal experiences and looking forward to the form and narrative that the architectural task should begin to take on. The design emanates from the superimposition of recalled and fictive images and the material-specific formulation and processing of a workpiece.

The particular and limiting characteristics of each material are revealed during the process of cutting and reassembling, taking on a clarifying role in answering narrative, spatial, and structural questions. Instead of an ill-fitting copy of a formal, preexisting, and already ingrained architectural concept, associative thinking and making are paramount. But beyond just developing an individual sense of expression and character, the spatial impact also needs to be verified in the end.

In the architectural design process, which is informed by the technical requirements of building, parallels with artistic work—a similarly author-based discipline—exist. Analogous to architecture, the fine arts are a cultural process in which a narrative exists and where materials are molded and deformed. In light of this, we invited a number of artists, for whom the process of making and its visible traces form an important part of the final work, to informal exchanges. While a sculptor usually ends his or her creative process with a physical object as the finished work of art, for architecture students the object as workpiece is just the beginning of the process. With each of the four artists whose work is featured in this book, we focused on different aspects and qualities of their approaches to making and predication.

For Alicja Kwade it is her alchemistry, like disassembling objects into individual components or materials that in return scrutinizes and reproduces their specific material properties. For Michael Beutler, it was his handcrafted machines and workbenches that not only fabricate art pieces with a self-evident traceability, but also become art works on their own part. For Eva Grubinger, it is her enlargement of unexceptional items to the scale of sculptures, which charges them with sudden, seismographic, and often minatorial meaning. For Isa Melsheimer, it is her instantaneous use of architecture as the starting point for her objects, where form, space, and scale convert into sculptures—seemingly the antidromic of our working process.

Together with my team, Nandini Oehlmann and Mathias Peppler, we have evolved a creative framework, the intermediate and final results of which are presented in the following pages as a loose compendium, without any intention of complete comprehensibility. Yet hopefully, while observing the variously beautiful, strange, and at times, even ugly objects, drawings, and models, some of the fortuitous coincidences and serendipitous surprises that arose from our speculations and actions will become apparent.

CRUSHING THINGS INTO MATTER

Alicja Kwade

Ein Gegenstand wird zermahlen

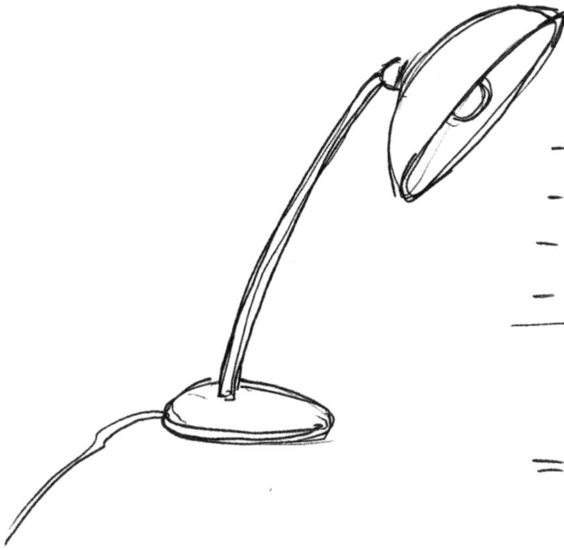

Lampe

2kg

- Eisen ca 1,6kg = spezifisches Gewicht = V
- Kunststoff ca. 0,3kg = spezifisches Gewicht = V
- Glas 0,05 kg = spezifischen Gewicht = V
- Messing 0,05 kg = spezifischen Gewicht = V

= V/X

Randstärke minimal

Schale

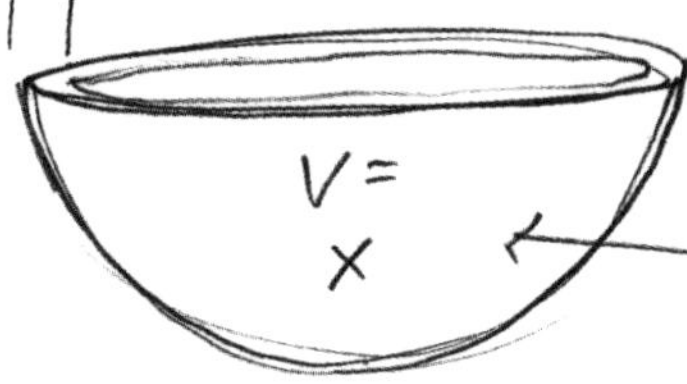

Lampenpulver + Epoxidharz. ca. 1/3 (wird aber noch ganz genau bestimmt.

Telefon iPhone

Eierbecher

stufig zerkleinert
, Fraktion < 2 mm
Nr : 9 von 14
Auftrag Nr
0346-14-03
, Berlin
Datum 11. Februar 2015
Bearbeiter Ulrich Bormann
Art der Probe
Kaiser-Tischlampe, mehrstufig zerkleinert
Außenlack, Fraktion < 2 mm
Menge: 6,2 g
Gebinde Nr : 10 von 14
Auftrag
Zerkleinerung Tischlampe „ROT"
Auftrag Nr
0346-14-03
Auftraggeber
Frau Alicja Kwade, Berlin
Datum 11. Februar 2015
Bearbeiter Ulrich Bormann
Art der Probe
Kaiser-Tischlampe, mehrstufig zerkleinert
Papier, Fraktion < 2 mm
Menge: 3,8 g
Gebinde Nr : 11 von 14
Auftrag
Zerkleinerung Tischlampe „ROT"
Auftrag Nr
0346-14-03
Auftraggeber
Frau Alicja Kwade, Berlin

ON OBJECTS

Bettina Kraus, Nandini Oehlmann, Mathias Peppler

MATERIAL AND CONSTRAINT

The exercises from which the objects emerged are essentially rudimentary prompts to do something, and above all specify boundary conditions with the intention of precluding certain decisions and making it easier to act. Their scope spans the actual question asked and the constraints inherent to each material—felt, wood, metal, stone, bamboo, hemp, turf—which subsequently become an integral part of the exercise and outcome. The result is a speculative space that can only be truly understood in hindsight when the object is analyzed and the question posed: What, in fact, is it? The established boundary conditions and material limitations, however, are not inhibitors, but rather catalysts for making intuitive decisions that help one move beyond preconceived notions or mental barriers. The boundary conditions preclude certain choices, narrow down the possibilities, and focus one's view. One could describe this with the term metamorphosis in the search for a form: The final state of the object is potentially already recorded in the material as part of its DNA.

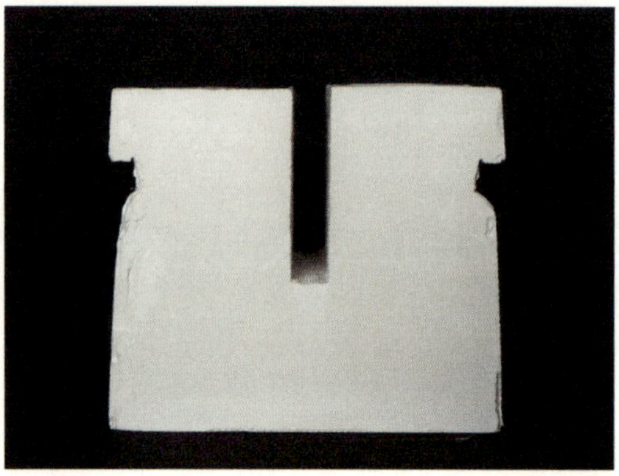

PURPOSE AND MEANING

We have come to expect that the things and people we meet in our daily encounters have a particular meaning or fulfill a specific purpose. Our world is a formatted one, in which we attempt to anticipate what each situation requires of us and how to use the things we come across. This formatting is useful in everyday life: It allows us to

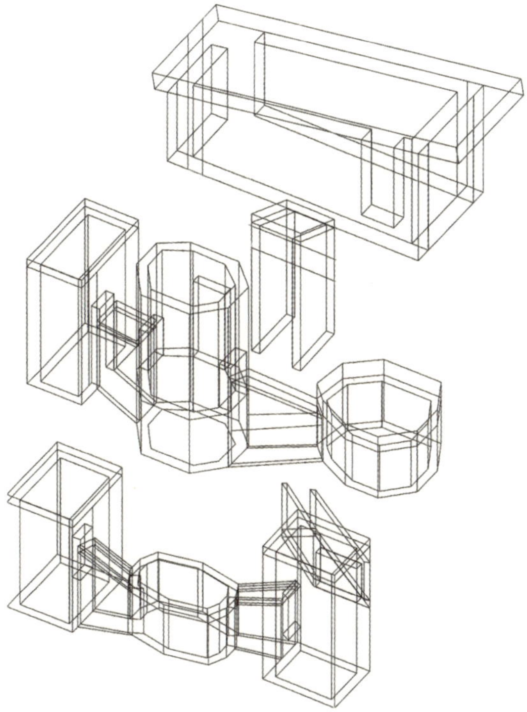

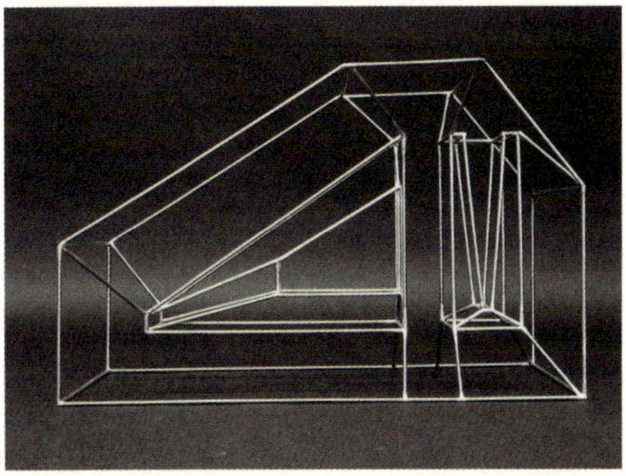

act appropriately and quickly find our orientation. We know what is expected of us, and are able to recognize the meaning correspondingly. Such a functional operating mode, however, is not free of external pressure, as the requirement to do something simultaneously demands a state of constant awareness.
It is a world we can ostensibly control and consists of messages and implications we attempt to decipher. And yet we perceive situations where this code is disrupted as particularly

authentic. We say we are taken back. In such moments, something that does not correspond with our expectations occurs and we have to observe everything more closely, and thus deviate from our default mode.

The objects provoke such instances. The simplicity of the task and the materials lead to self-contained constructs, which adhere to no specific purpose and have no higher meaning. They simply exist and remain peculiarly complete because they have no specific subtext. This situation is one that we rarely encounter, and one that may be best described as "presence." Neither of an artistic nor utilitarian nature, the objects simply demand that their existence be recognized. At first glance, the interplay between the material and how they were made indicates that they are simple entities whose complexity is only revealed upon further consideration. In general, their appeal may simply be to look closer.

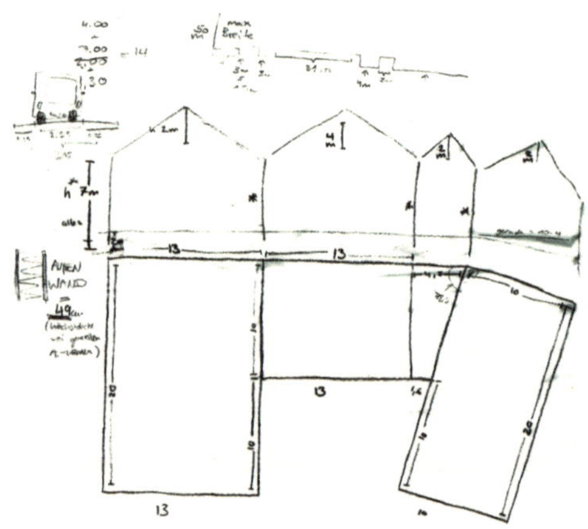

FAULTS AND TRACES

Surprisingly, it is not only the evident choices within the objects that are comprehensible, but also their faults, which cannot be immediately deduced from the rest of the construct or their style. Although it is almost impossible to find overriding explanations for these faults, they do not seem out of key. Instead, they are a self-explanatory part of the entire piece, remnants of the path followed apart from a systematic decision-making process—be they spontaneous inspirations, technical mishaps, or irregularities already present in the raw material that leave their mark on the finished object. Thus, the objects are entities in which the systematic and happenstance overlap and (can) seem plausible within its own microcosm. This may be due to the plain fact that it was possible, nothing prevented it from occurring, or that it was already present from the beginning. In a sense it is a naive method, but also one that elicits a desire to act. And within the isolated world of the object it seems innately authentic and thus intelligible.

The objects are therefore comprehensible and transparent entities, in which not only a variety of decisions coexist, but also, when taken together as the result of a single creative process, overlap and necessitate the existence of one another. As elementary as the objects and their production methods sometimes are, and as comprehensible their effect may seem, they are that much more difficult to explain. “By this definition, the transparent ceases to be that which is perfectly clear and becomes instead that which is clearly ambiguous” (Colin Rowe and Robert Slutzky, *Transparency: Literal and Phenomenal,* 1963, p.45). In a simplistic way, they are testament to the fact that comprehensibility is not only singlehandedly achieved through explanatory means, but also reveals it to be a phenomenon with the potential to be understood visually—in this case evoked through the authenticity of what has taken place and the traces left behind.

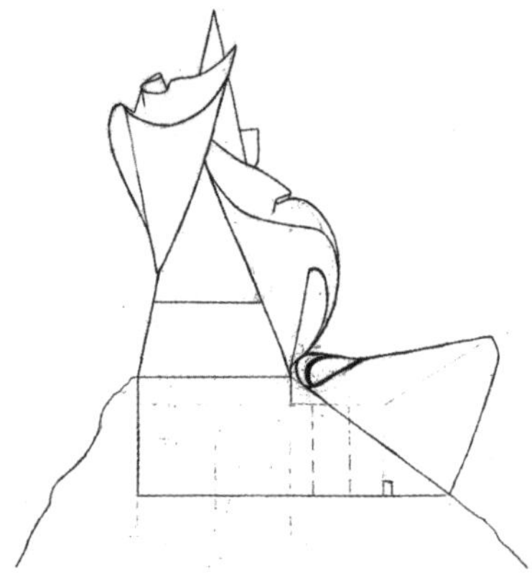

TABLES

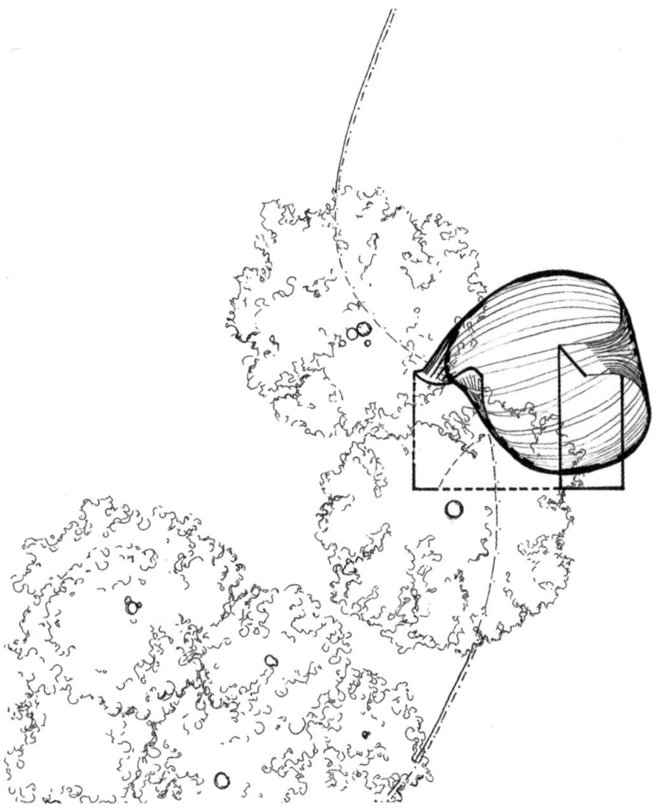

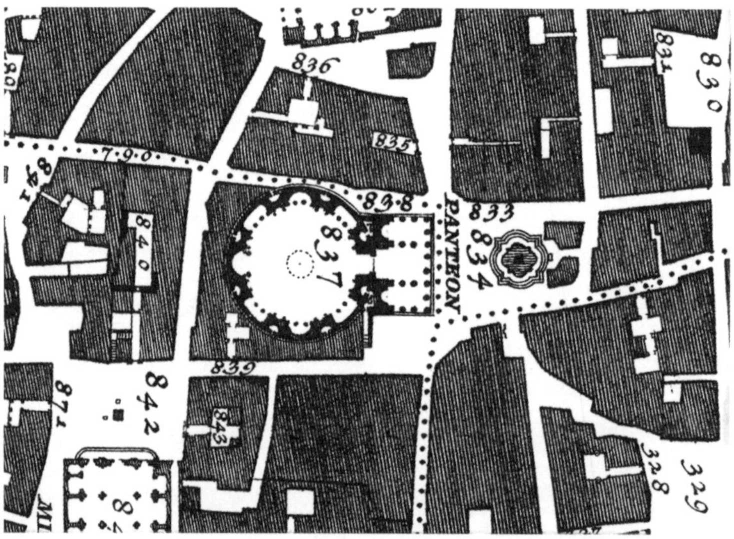
836
835
830
833
PANTHEON
834
837
840
839
842
843
328
329

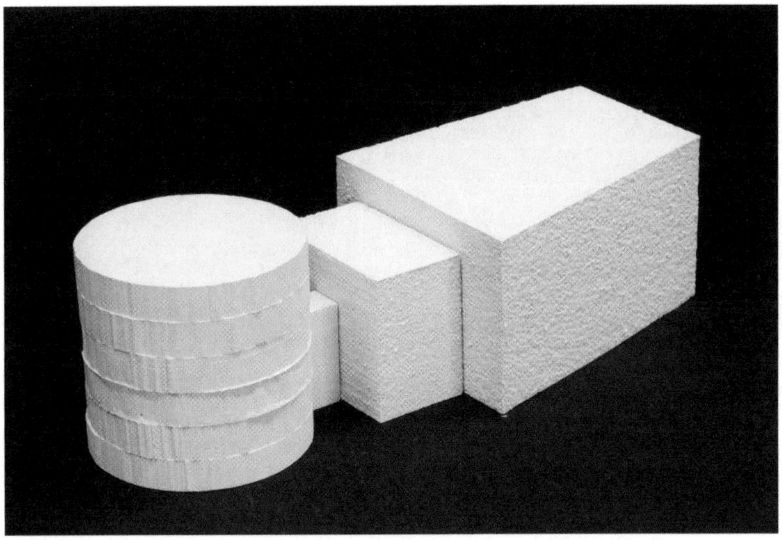

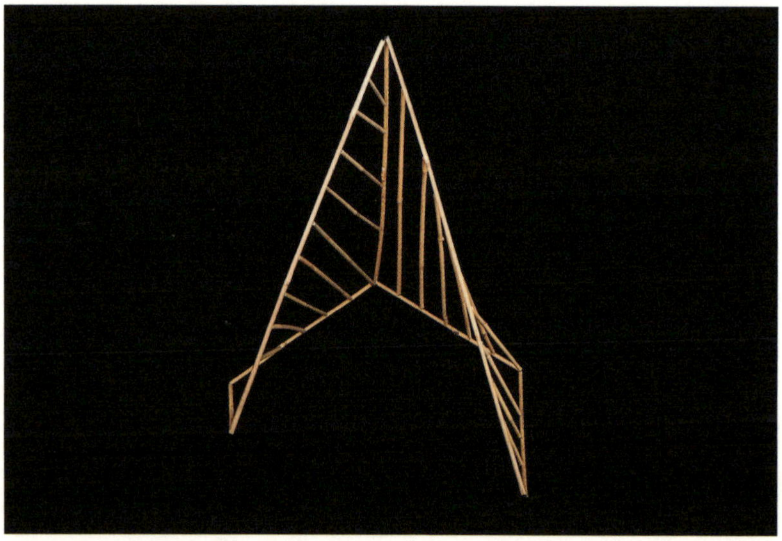

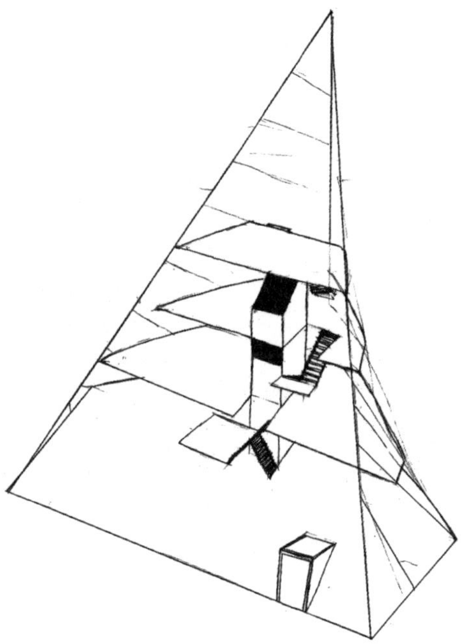

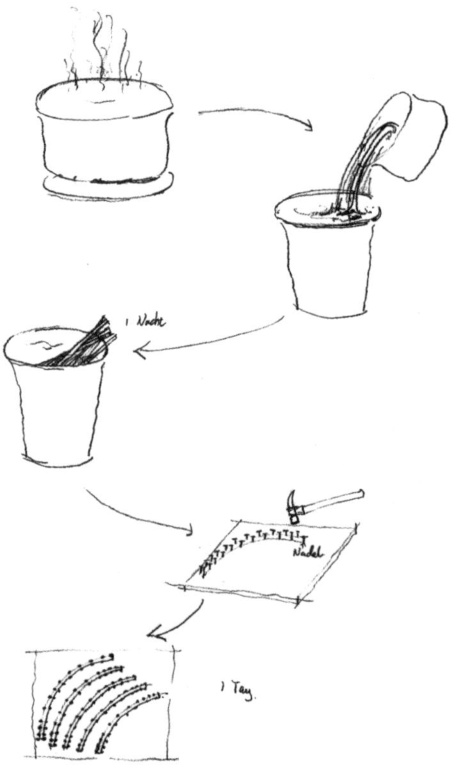
1 Nacht
Nadel
1 Tag.

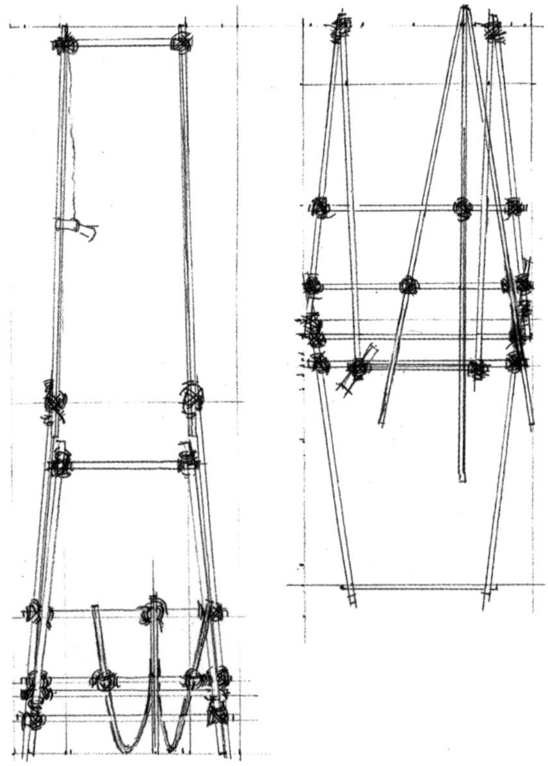

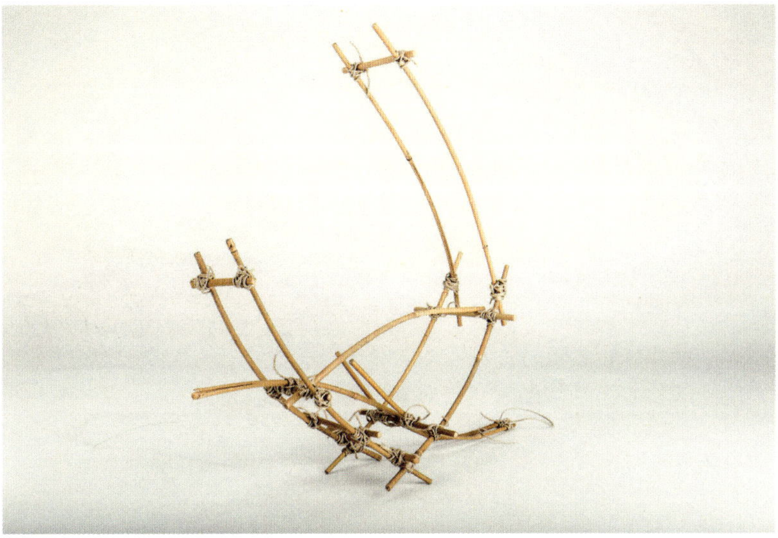

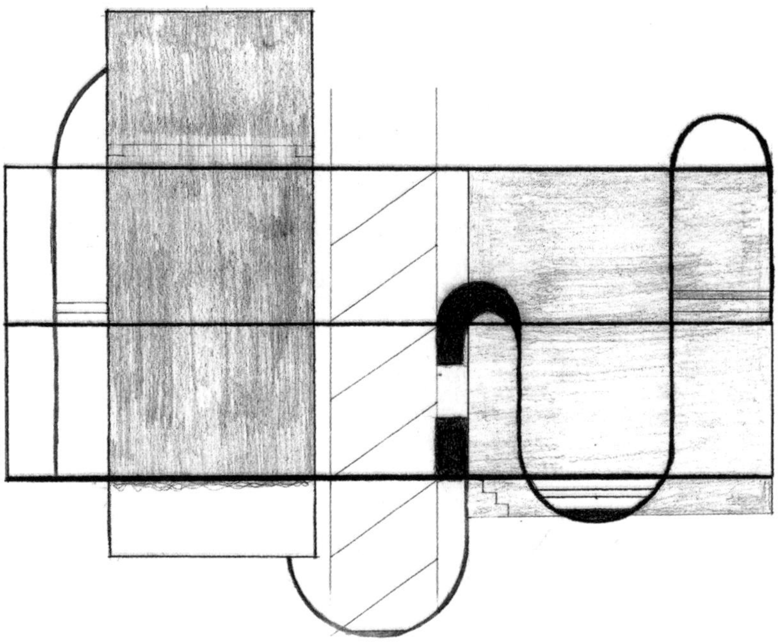

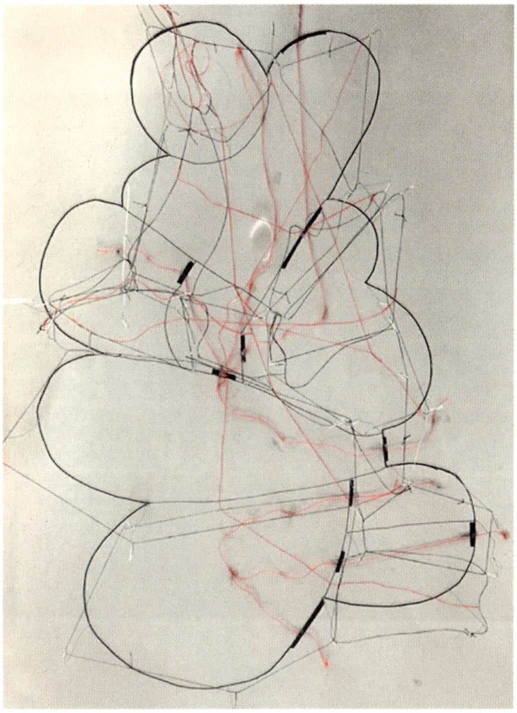

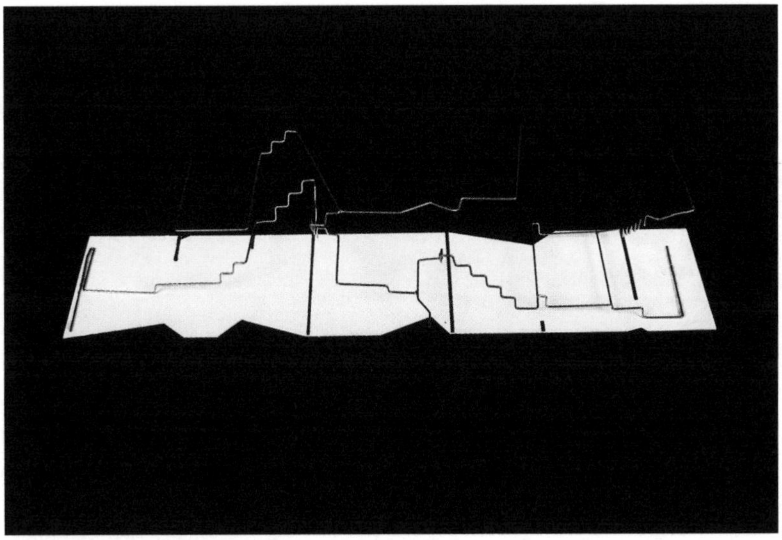

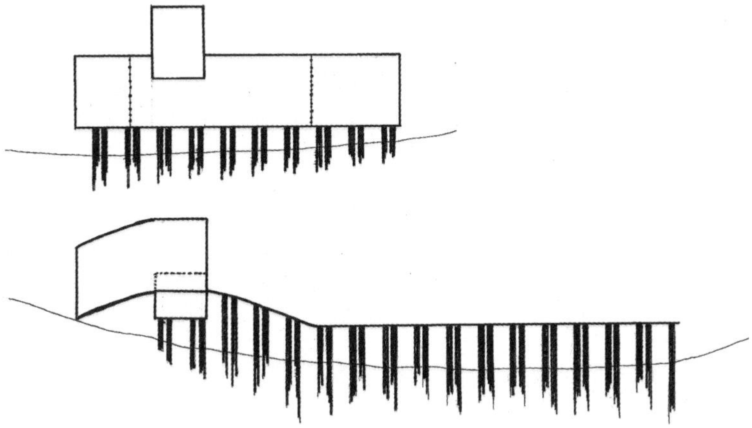

Michael Beutler

„Rustika – kommt die 0 zur 8" → at: KESTNER GESELLSCHAFT, HANNOVER 2007 and: BONNIERS KONSTHALL 2008

and „Tea factory" → at: Spike Island, Bristol and: Nottingham Contemporary 2016

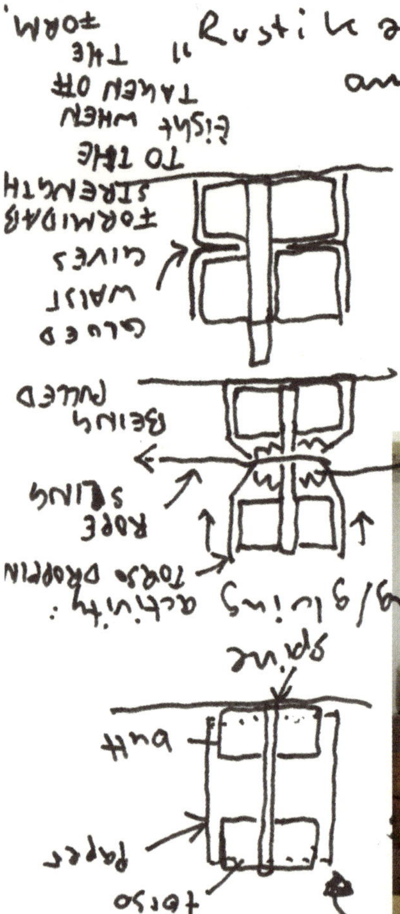

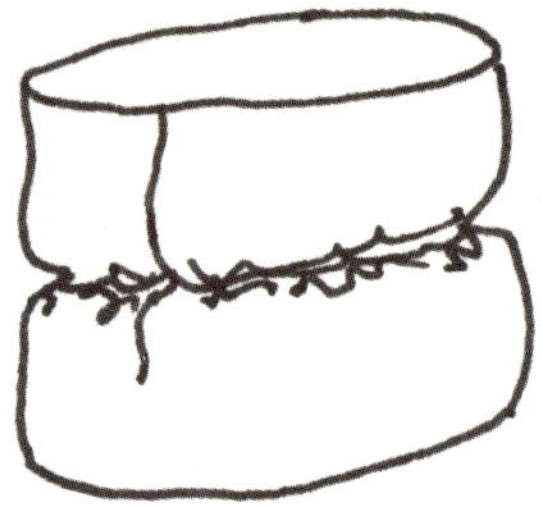

② How that shape is made: there is this joke: a Zero meets an Eight on the street and says: „What an amazing belt you have!" → this is the technical principal to make this work

① The work was originally develloped to fill a designated space within the Kestner Gesellschafts MAIN exhibition hall. The building was once a public indoor swimming pool. Arcades which defined ~~my~~ space, were running along one side of the big pool.

I was offered this slightly odd, tucked in space. Maybe because it reminded me ~~of~~ a wine-cellar or the great opening scene of the muppet show in which all the monster pop up in their designated Gate on stage. These two impressions guided me to find these types of barrel-like paper bodies.

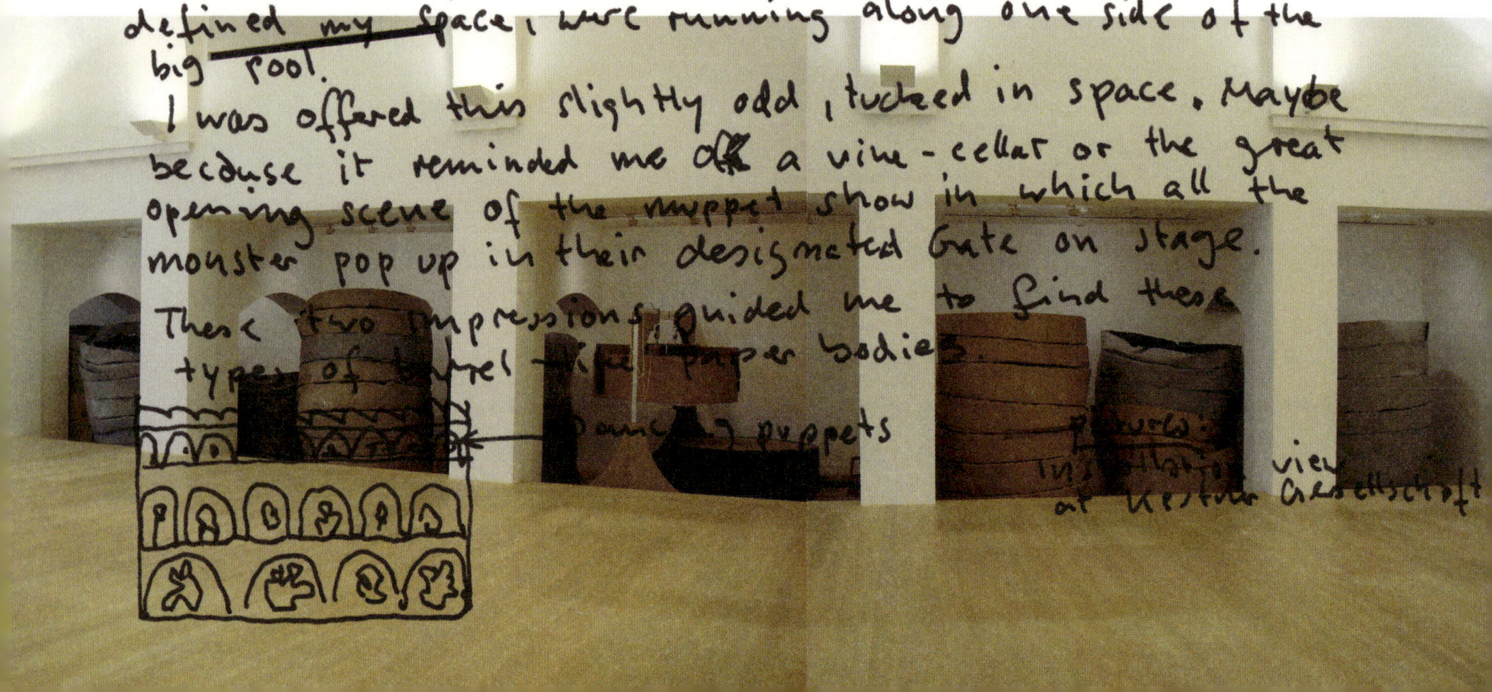

Dancing puppets

artwork: installation view at Kestner Gesellschaft

DURING THE PRODUCTION

DEMONSTRATION OF STRUCTURAL STRENGTH

PROTECTIVE WEAR

THE EXHIBITION-SITE TURNED INTO WORKSHOP

CRANE WITHOUT SPINE

DRYING RINGS

TORSO

very important: enormous amounts of glue

THE PIECES HAVE TO BE PRODUCED ON SITE, SINCE THE PAPER RINGS ARE TO FRAGILE TO BE TRANSPORTED.

DIFFERENT TYPES OF PAPERS ARE BEING PRESSED. THE PRODUCTION IS AN ONGOING EXPERIMENT

These two pages show the manual, that i have written to pass on the knowlegde of this specific craft.

Rustika / kommt die 0 zur 8

The System

Material

1. Resources
Any type of cardboard, thick paper, felt, one-sided corrugated paper, all come in rolls of a minimum width of ca 1 m, maximum width approx. 160 cm. The bigger the variety, the better.

2. Refined material
a. In stock: All that is produced gets destroyed.
b. Respectively produced: Rings of the different materials of a diameter of 140 cm and different widths.

Crew

Three people are needed to operate the device and carry around the very fragile freshly produced rings.

Other tools

A lot of wood glue is needed (approx. 1 liter/kg per ring), cutter, hand stapler, staples, sheets to protect the floor from glue.

The device

1. Parts
A cardboard core pipe of 2 m length, a standing drum with a diameter of 140 cm, height 60 cm, a drum of the same dimensions hanging from two pulleys on a two-footed crane on little wheels, a rope, a stool, an unrolling handle, three metal hand-shovels, one glue spatula. >

2. Set up of the device

The crane is put together with the given bolts. Hang pulleys and hanging drum onto the crane. Lift up the crane and move it over the standing drum. There should be enough space, so that both drums can stand next to each other.

I made this manual in the occasion of my exhibition at Bonniers Konsthall, Stockholm in 2008. I was wondering if it was possible to install this work, without me being there.

Use of the device

Step one: Move the hanging drum over the standing one and let it down. Put the long core pipe all the way down to the ground into the hole in the middle of the drums. To do so, move the crane slightly to one side.

Step two: Put a roll of cardboard on the dispenser handle. While one person holds this, another one unrolls the paper around the drums. Cut the paper with the cutter with about 30 to 40 cm overlap. Stretch it around the drums and fix the ends together with the staple gun (this works best where the drum-walls have gaps). Fix the paper with the stick needles (the little things attached to the hanging drum), then two people lift the hanging drum and the attached paper with the pulleys all the way to the cross beam. The pulleys get locked in this position, so that the people can do something else.

Step three: Put glue on the paper in the area of the gap in between the two drums. More is better than less. The shovels will be useful.

Step four: When all sides are covered, two people get hold of the pulleys while the third binds the rope like a sling around the middle of the paper. While the others slowly let down the hanging drum, the rope person accordingly pulls the sling like tightening a belt, so that the paper ring gets a waist until the drums sit on each other again. Just before they meet, the rope should be pulled out. One person climbs onto the drums (here the stool is very useful), jumps around a little to put some pressure on the paper and pulls out the core pipe. It might be the case that the others have to shake the device a little to make it easier.

The pipe is put to one side, the person climbs back onto the floor again, the needles are taken out from the paper and the upper drum is pulled up carefully above the paper, fixed and moved to the side with the whole crane. >

Step five: The three people take off the paper ring from the standing drum, by lifting it up tenderly, holding both the upper and the lower section of the paper ring. They move the ring to a safe place where it can dry.

Installation

Location

The system was first developed for a Jugendstil swimming hall turned exhibition space. The work was shown in a side wing of the main gallery and mainly reacted to architectural details of the site: Square frames facing the main space and arches supporting the lower ceiling inside the wing. These elements are echoed in the round and flat rings. They could be barrels in a wine cellar. If these shapes happen to be in the exhibition context, it might be a nice coincidence, but else it is mainly important to have enough space to let the fresh rings dry. This is a work for the inside.

Rules and behaviour

It is very likely that one ring seems to turn out like another. When working in a flow, it took 8–13 minutes to produce a ring. Drying takes much longer. This may become boring after a while, but since the rings are really fragile when not yet dry, something exciting is going on when handling them and taking them off the drum. Nothing speaks against painterly activities when gluing the paper. Good style drops are welcome. When the first few rings have been produced, it makes sense to have a look at them and search for differences and figure out how they occurred.

Size

Basic space requirements: The space for production and space for exhibition are very different in this case. While loads of space is needed to produce and to dry the rings, it all takes little space when the rings are stacked. The first room was about 60 m^2 big and not very high (just 2.30 m). The production place was at least six times larger than that.

Display and construction

Making nice rings comes first and then piling up nice columns. A variety can be found in this way, how symmetrical the rings are produced or not, how the glue flows. The columns can have glue dots running upwards; the rings of paper can be stacked onto each other or around each other. It is useful to look at how long a column stays stable. The stronger the material, the higher the column can be. No ring should be wasted and end up totally flattened inside a column.

The positioning of the columns depends very much on the given architecture. Since they are self supportive, something is gained when they stand on their own, or at least at such a distance that one can walk around them. It may not matter if the columns are positioned in a certain grid or just put to one side like material that gets used every now and then. An installation should be made out of at least 40 rings.

Deconstruction

The rings are far too fragile to transport and take too much space when stored, so all the columns and rings are destroyed after an exhibition. The material can go back into paper recycling. The device and all parts of it including the stool are kept.

Documentation

Video: some mpeg movies from the production time in Hanover.
Exhibited: "Made in Germany",
Kestner Gesellschaft Hannover, 2007;
"Verwendungsnachweis", MMK Frankfurt am Main 2007.

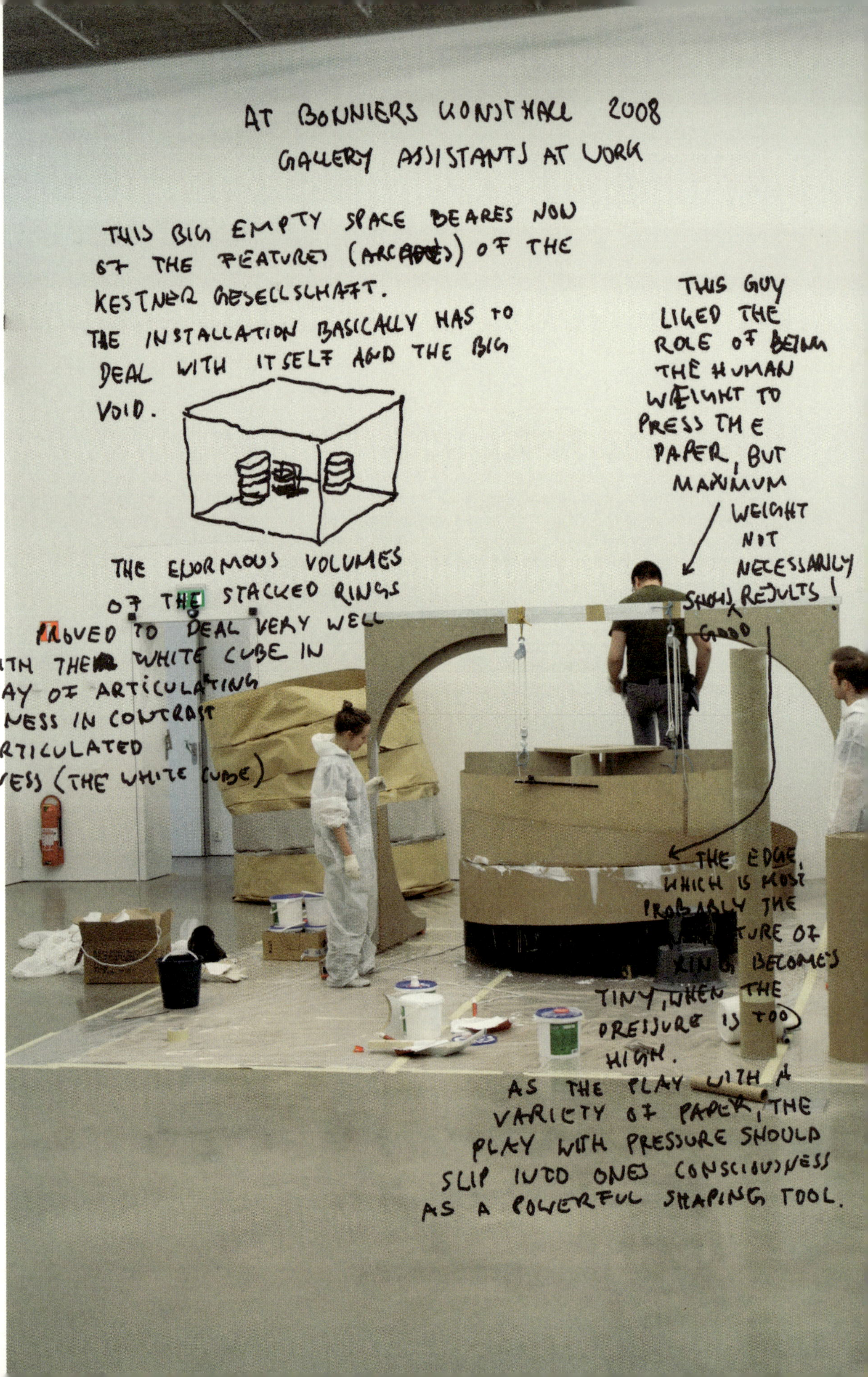
AT BONNIERS KONSTHALL 2008
GALLERY ASSISTANTS AT WORK
THIS BIG EMPTY SPACE BEARES NOW OF THE FEATURES (ARCADES) OF THE KESTNER GESELLSCHAFT.
THE INSTALLATION BASICALLY HAS TO DEAL WITH ITSELF AND THE BIG VOID.
THE ENORMOUS VOLUMES OF THE STACKED RINGS PROVED TO DEAL VERY WELL WITH THE WHITE CUBE IN A WAY OF ARTICULATING EMPTINESS IN CONTRAST TO UNARTICULATED EMPTINESS (THE WHITE CUBE)
THIS GUY LIKED THE ROLE OF BEING THE HUMAN WEIGHT TO PRESS THE PAPER, BUT MAXIMUM WEIGHT NOT NECESSARILY SHOWS GOOD RESULTS!
THE EDGE, WHICH IS MOST PROBABLY THE FEATURE OF THE RING BECOMES TINY, WHEN THE PRESSURE IS TOO HIGH.
AS THE PLAY WITH A VARIETY OF PAPER, THE PLAY WITH PRESSURE SHOULD SLIP INTO ONES CONSCIOUSNESS AS A POWERFUL SHAPING TOOL.

Rustika / kommt die 0 zur 8
27.2. – 16.3.2008
A POSTER ON THE WALL SHOWS THE FINAL RESULT OF THIS INSTALLATION WITHOUT MY PRESENCE.
SIGNS OF COLLAPSING. THE MAXIMUM HEIGHT OF THIS BARREL IS REACHED
TINY CRACK
DIFFERENT PAPERS

„RUSTIKA - KOMMT DIE 0 ZUR 8" TRANSFORMED INTO A SPACE FRAME SYSTEM: „TEA FACTORY".
THE TECHNICAL PRINCIPLE („WAISTING") OF „RUSTIKA" WAS ADOPTED TO A SINGLE (ACTUALLY THREE) SIMILAR TYPE OF PAPER, WHICH WE HAD FOUND ON A SCRAP YARD IN THE SUBURBS OF BRISTOL.
THE STRUCTURE WE HAD BUILD HERE RESEMBLES THE ARCHITECTURAL SKELETON OF THE BUILDING WHICH WAS ONCE A TEA-PACKING FACTORY!
THE DIAMETER IS SMALLER WHICH MAKES THE COLUMNS STRONGER. THERE ARE ALSO TWO DIFFERENT DIAMETERS TO SOFTEN THE RELATIONSHIP BETWEEN VOLUMES
SMALLER
BIGGER
EXTRA FEATURES WERE ADDED TO THE DRESSES TO MAKE CROSS-PIECES AND ARCH-PIECES.
„THE TEA FACTORY"
SPIKE ISLAND, BRISTOL
2016
FOTO: STUAR

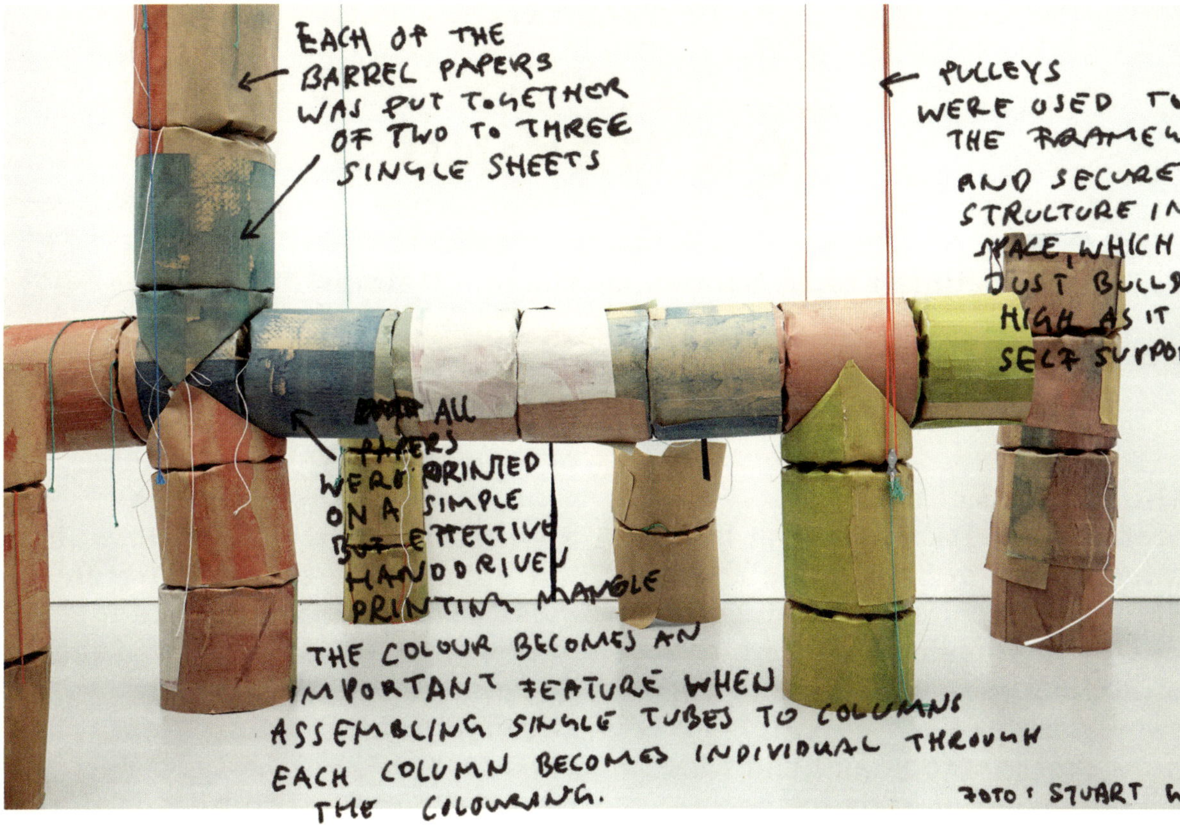
EACH OF THE BARREL PAPERS WAS PUT TOGETHER OF TWO TO THREE SINGLE SHEETS
PULLEYS WERE USED TO ERECT THE FRAMEWORK AND SECURE THE STRUCTURE IN SPACE, WHICH WAS JUST BUILD AS HIGH AS IT WAS SELF SUPPORTING
ALL PAPERS WERE PRINTED ON A SIMPLE BUT EFFECTIVE HANDDRIVEN PRINTING MANGLE
THE COLOUR BECOMES AN IMPORTANT FEATURE WHEN ASSEMBLING SINGLE TUBES TO COLUMNS EACH COLUMN BECOMES INDIVIDUAL THROUGH THE COLOURING.
FOTO: STUART WHIPPS

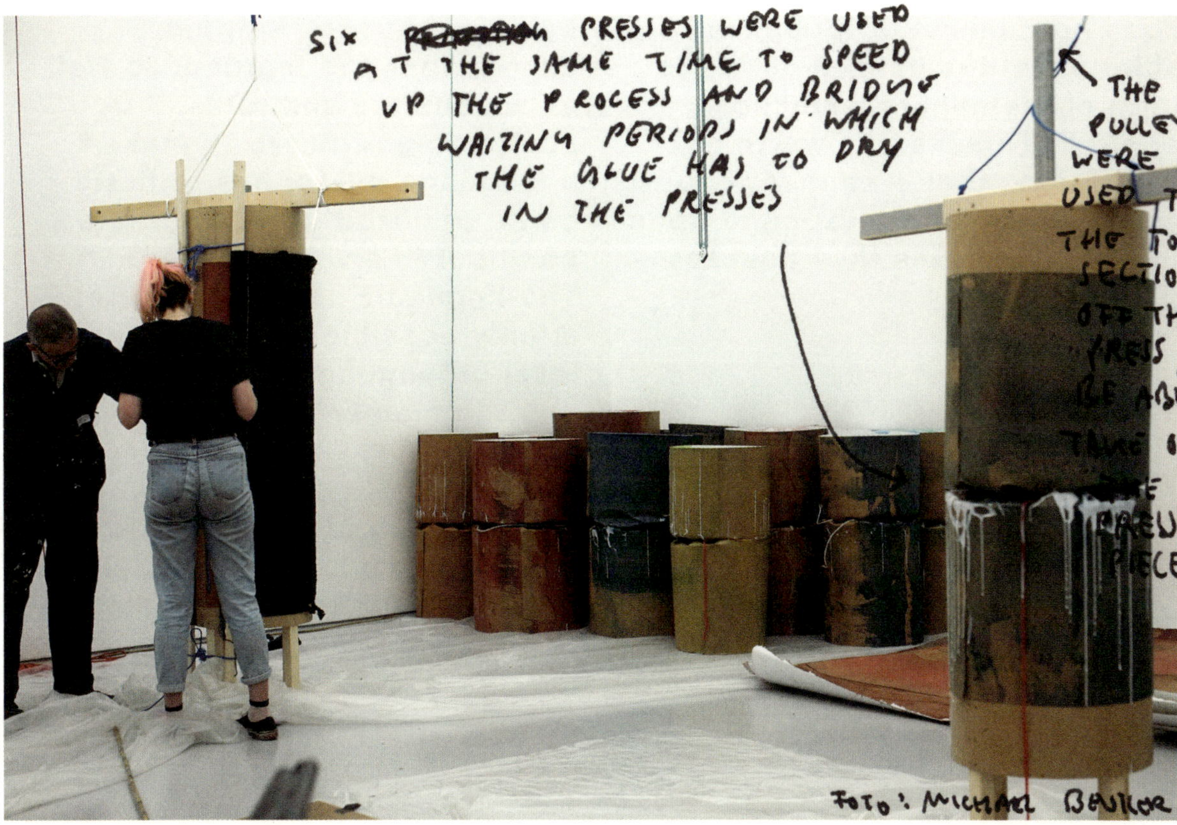
SIX PRESSES WERE USED AT THE SAME TIME TO SPEED UP THE PROCESS AND BRIDGE WAITING PERIODS IN WHICH THE GLUE HAS TO DRY IN THE PRESSES
THE PULLEYS WERE ALSO USED TO LIFT THE TOP SECTION OFF THE PRESS TO BE ABLE TO TAKE OUT THE PRESSED PIECE
FOTO: MICHAEL BENKER

ON MAKING

Bettina Kraus, Nandini Oehlmann, Mathias Peppler

INTUITION AND COINCIDENCE

The practice of teaching architecture takes place at the intersection of knowledge and ability. In architectural education, design is classically taught in studio courses with a focus on semester-long projects. It is here that methods and skills are imparted directly to the participants. However, a significant portion of the knowledge conveyed does not consist of formalized abilities, but is passed on in the form of metaphors, sketches, or similar means. It's worth mentioning that even many experts are often unable to expound upon the competencies they possess, or how they apply such skills or knowledge. Therefore, the production of knowledge in architecture has little to do with the praxis, where one operates mostly with implied knowledge. In line with Polyani's idea of tacit knowledge, the knower and the knowledge form a single entity.

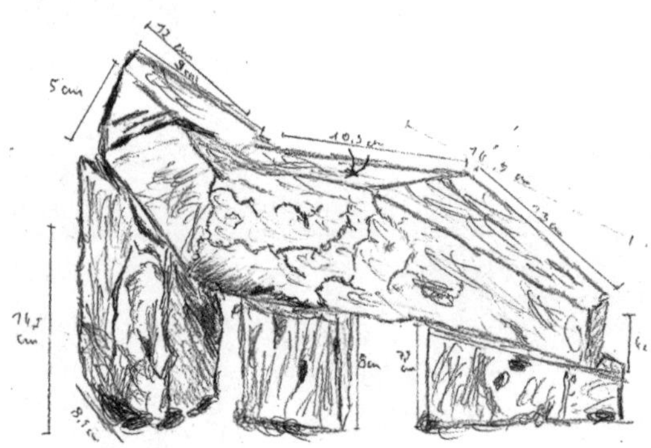

A useful comparison here is the process of learning a language, which is similarly one of learning by doing. At first, singular expressions are learned, as well as vocabulary and rules. The scaffolding required to make a language useful has to first be internalized in order to later handle it in a virtuoso manner. The linguistic artistry of literature is only possible with a higher level of language competency, and the moment of turning words into literature is an epiphanous one. Our ability to use language is comprised of the interplay between cognitive knowledge and intuition. When speaking or writing, complex grammatical rules are intuitively applied to form correct sentences without the need to actively recall the applicable rules. This is in fact how a native language is implicitly acquired.

By comparison, in architectural education this process is often replaced with the search for a concept to illustrate a thought. During the design process, and analogous to language, it is possible to develop a feeling for how the parts can be best combined to form a whole. One could even view (physical) experiences and our dealings with gravity, space, and the built environment as a kind of experiential, a priori knowledge incidentally accrued during the activities of everyday life. And this knowledge can be called upon when designing spaces and structures. Or, through repetition, a rule can be internalized until it can be applied with ease: “All skills, even the most abstract begin as bodily practices” and “knowledge is gained in the hand through touch and movement” (Richard Sennett, *The Craftsman*, 2008, p. 10). In other words, understanding is by way of the hands.

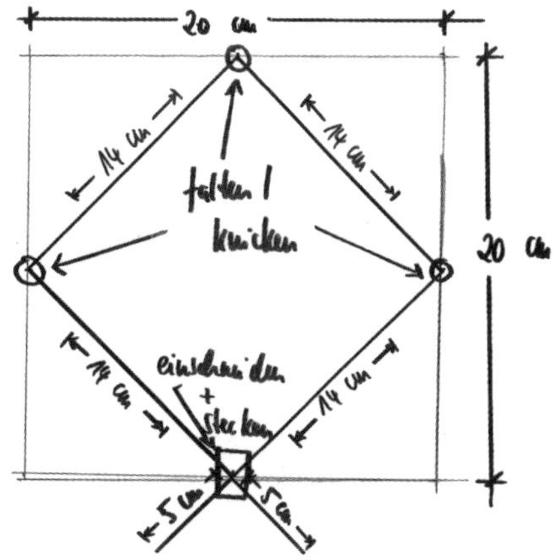

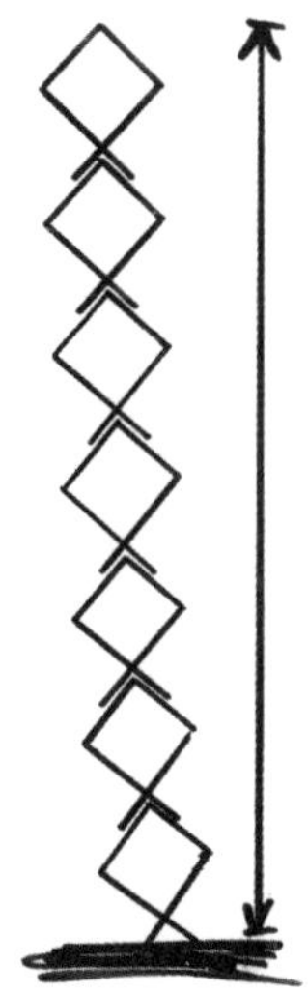

FRAGMENTS AND COLLISIONS

Once started, our design process is starkly fragmented into smaller subtasks. Each excerpt focuses on only part of the final design and is dealt with individually—an approach that aims to generate moments of varying complexity and improve one’s capability to act. However, it goes without saying that when these excerpts are combined a succession of collisions between the existing and new arises. The unintentional and the happenstance that necessarily result from these collisions are of particular importance here. By removing parts of the whole, complexity is reduced and an operating space is generated where one can pursue a more focused working method. Similar to looking through a microscope, the focus shifts from the macro- to the microcosm. Control over the situation in its entirety is set aside for a moment, so that something new and free from outside influence can emerge. When the existing collides with the new, one has to zoom out and again regain control.

This constant back and forth, zooming in and out, is an enriching process, and one that demands losing sight of the whole picture, and thus relinquishing control. Learning to design in this way is like learning to observe more precisely in order to detect and identify fortuitous coincidences. A language with the ability to best anticipate and guide these actions is necessarily simple and precise. Accordingly, the assignments are formatted and divided into individual sections and procedural steps. With each additional step, a new design parameter is introduced, increasing the intricacy of the task in a way that takes into account the complexity of dealing with architecture. During this cycle of action, appropriation, and understanding, the object becomes a house.

DIFFERENCE AND SURPLUS

It is difficult to theoretically anticipate the final results and their impact when working by hand, and an unintentional and unpredictable surplus almost inevitably arises somewhere between what we already know and what materializes in the end. There exists a difference between the intended outcome and the actual result. And the extent of this indeterminate surplus is dependent on a number of factors, including the manner in which the object was produced, manual and other personal skills, the material, and the complexity of the idea. The initial exercises, which led to the development of the objects, are rudimentary in their explanations of what is expected and seemingly useless in establishing a possible overarching set of goals. In a minimally simplistic way, a maximally complex form is created—and in a much shorter period of time than would be necessary for a more theoretical working process.

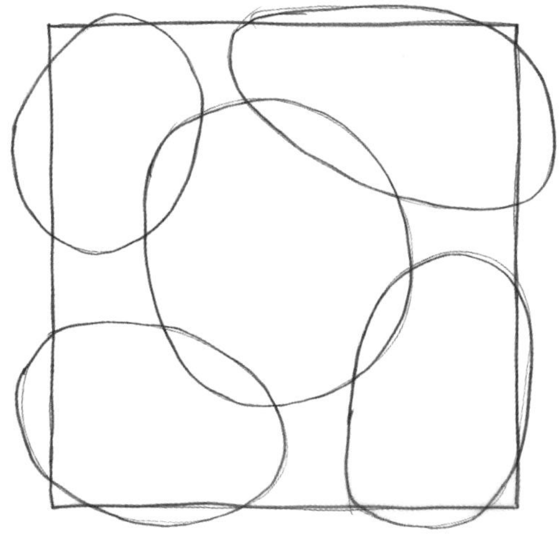

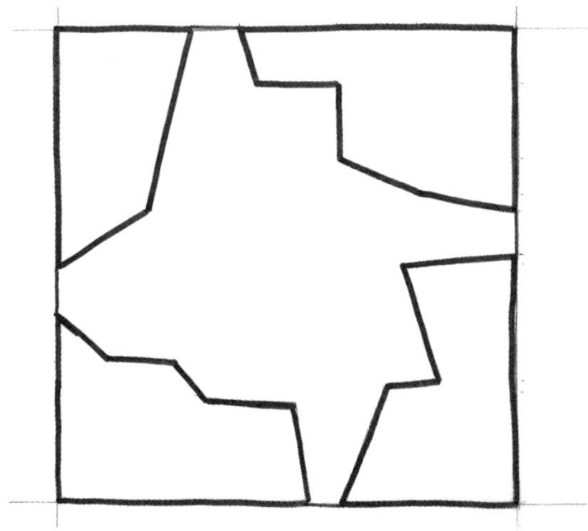

After the initial step, the prompts call much less for an additive method of working and much more for an understanding of what this difference between intention and reality actually is. The term "serendipity" can be described as the surprise discovery of something originally not sought, but arrived at after careful and in-depth observation, and can be applied quite accurately to describe a portion of the work with the objects. The reflective work that follows is therefore a design-based reappraisal, which at its core generates a constant contextual analysis. It is a design process, which above all else is directed at refining the skills of observation.

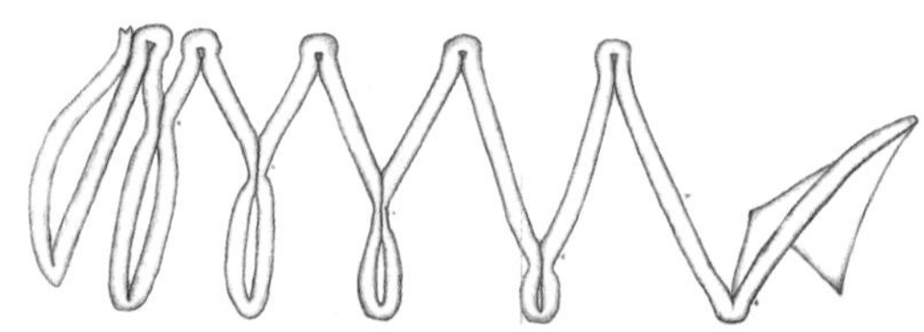

TABLES

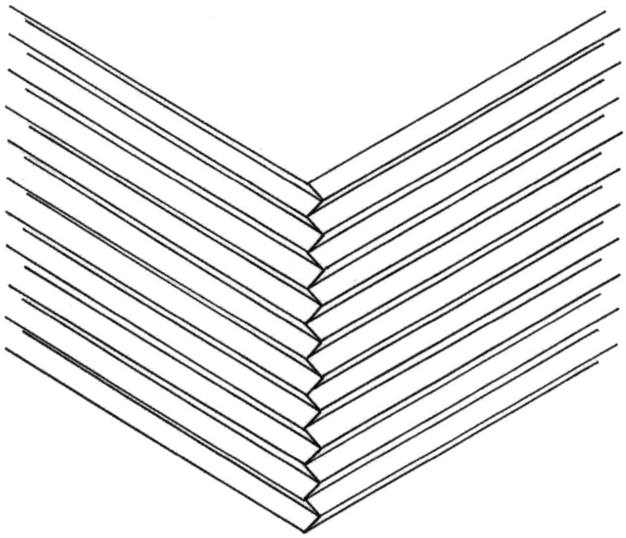

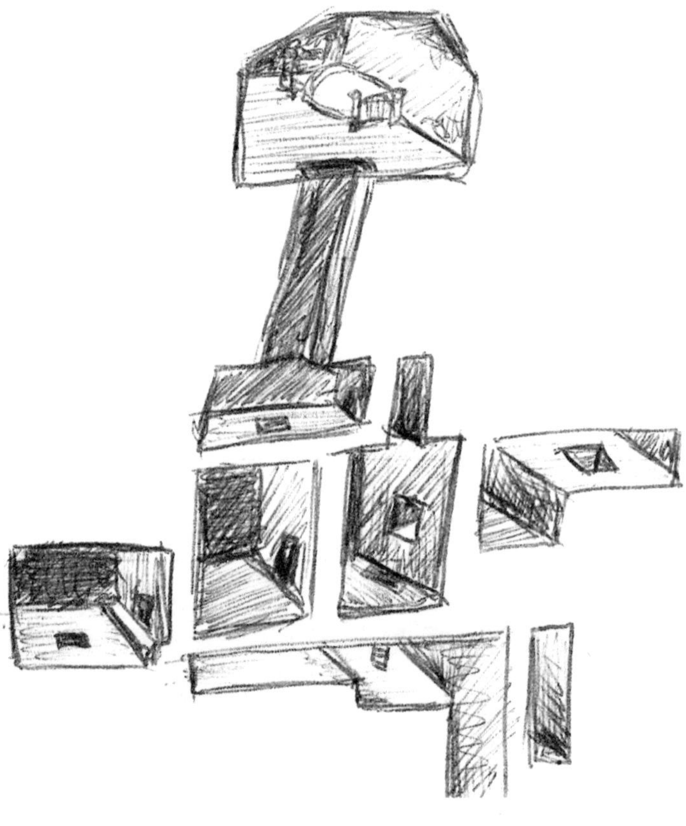

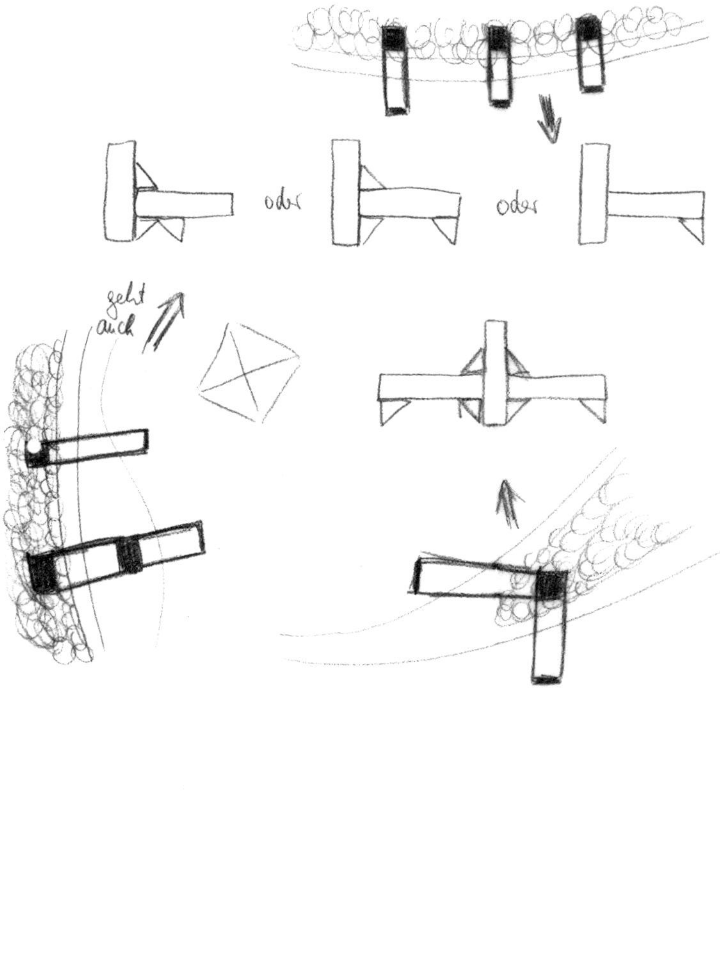
oder
oder
geht auch

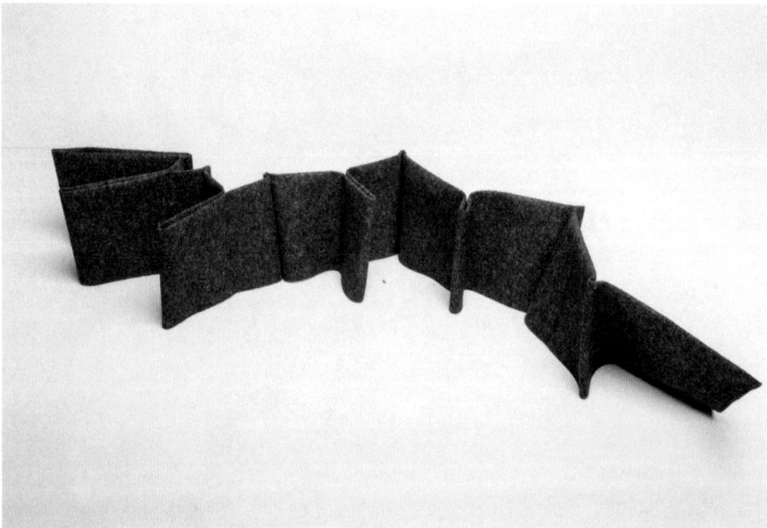

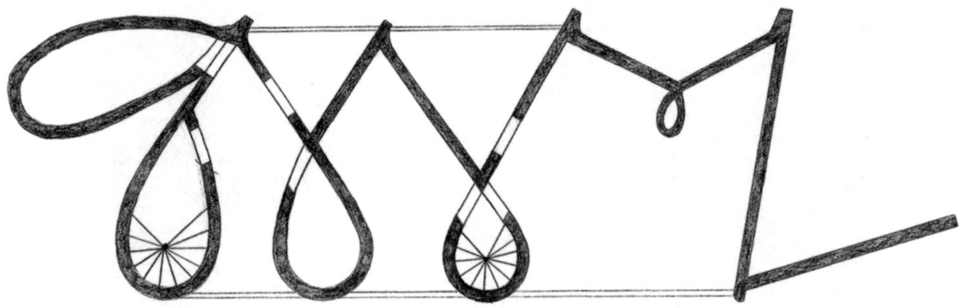

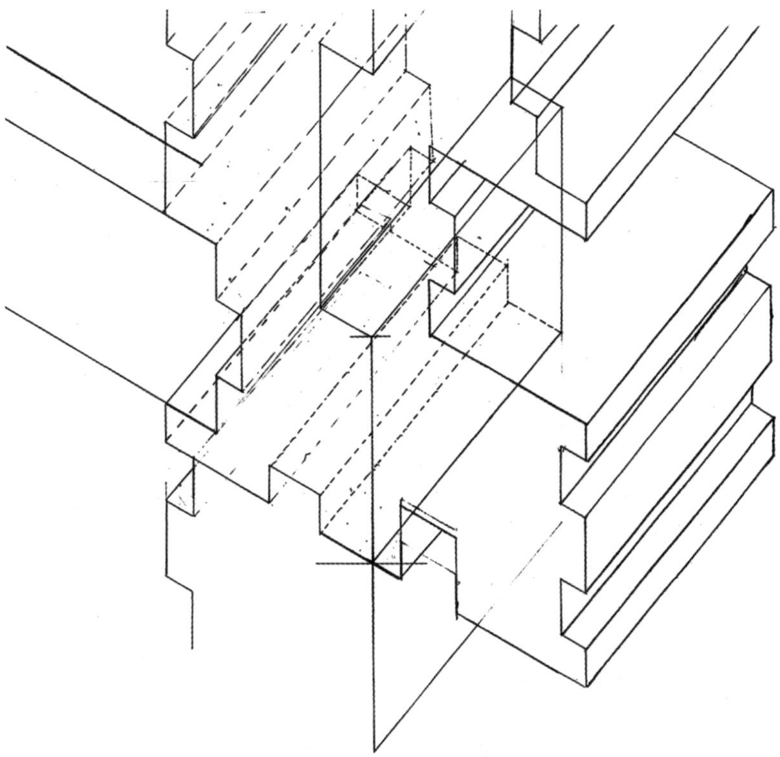

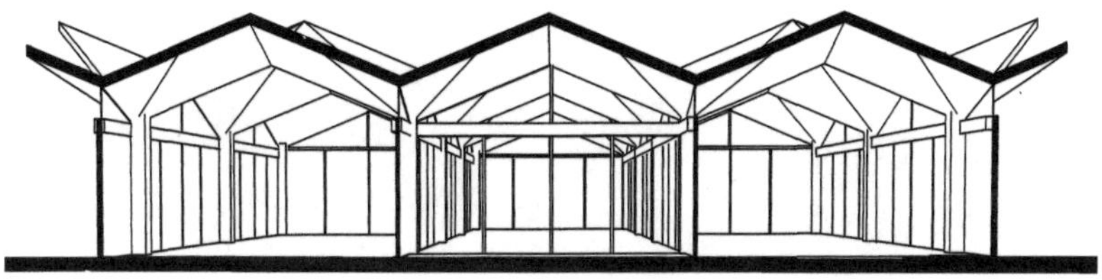

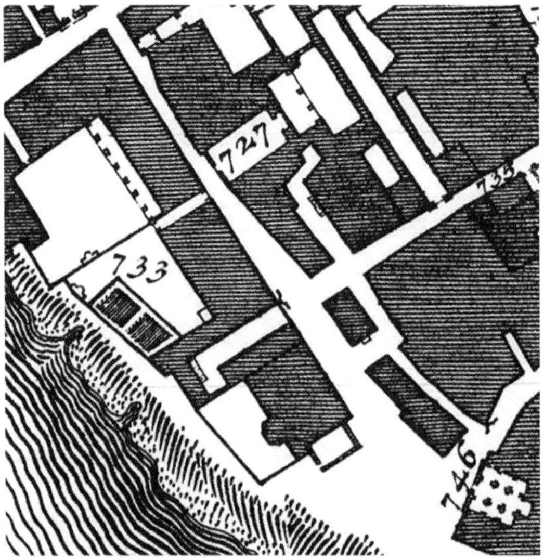
727
733
746

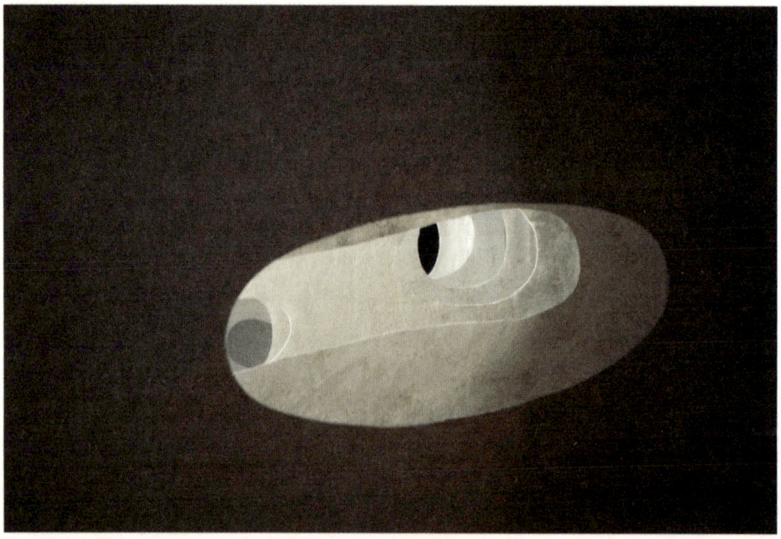

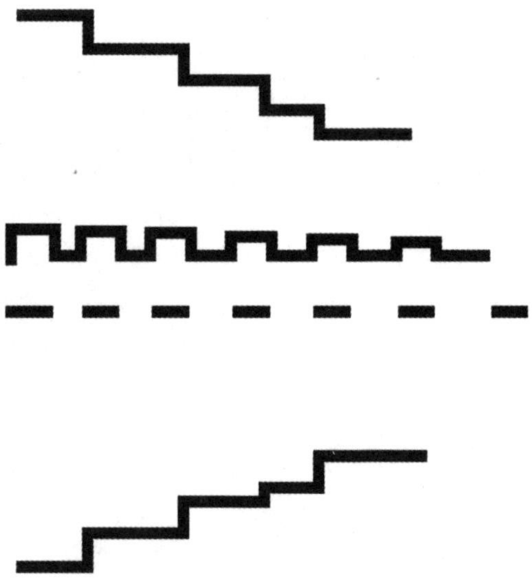

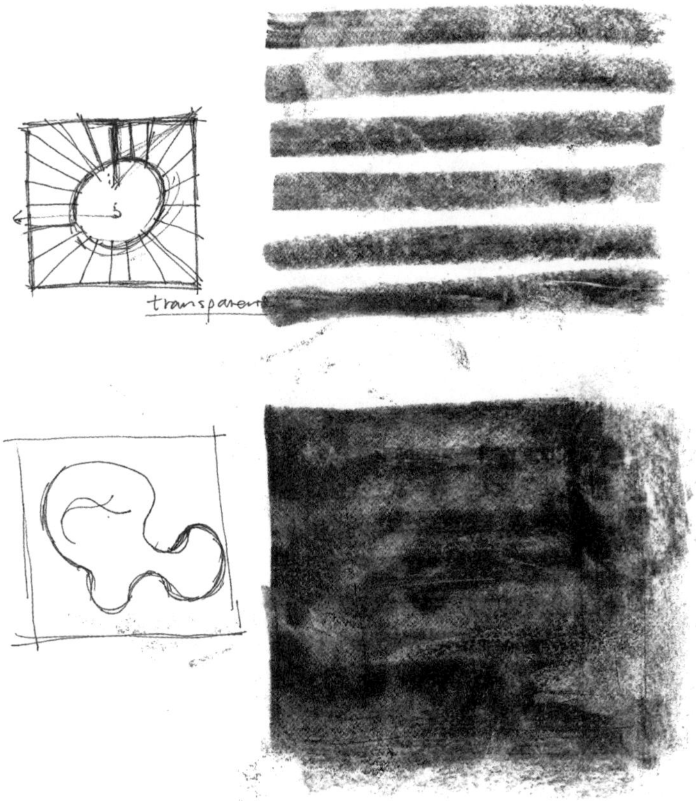

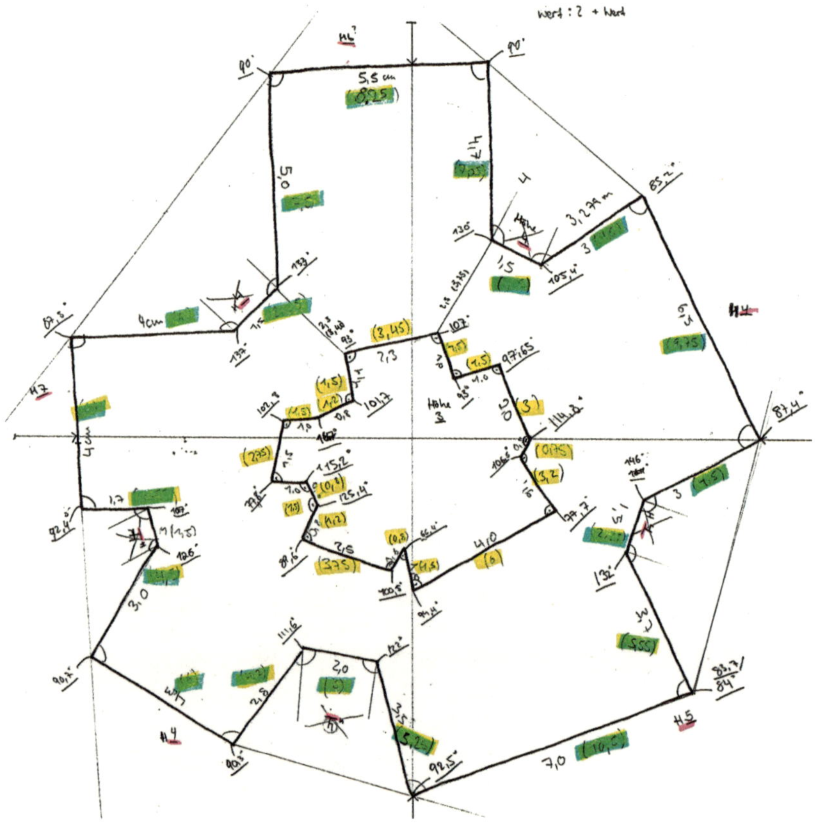

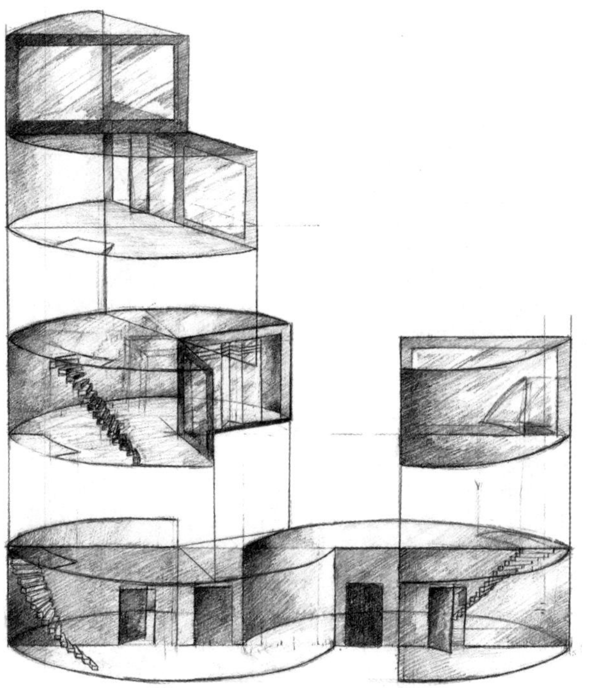

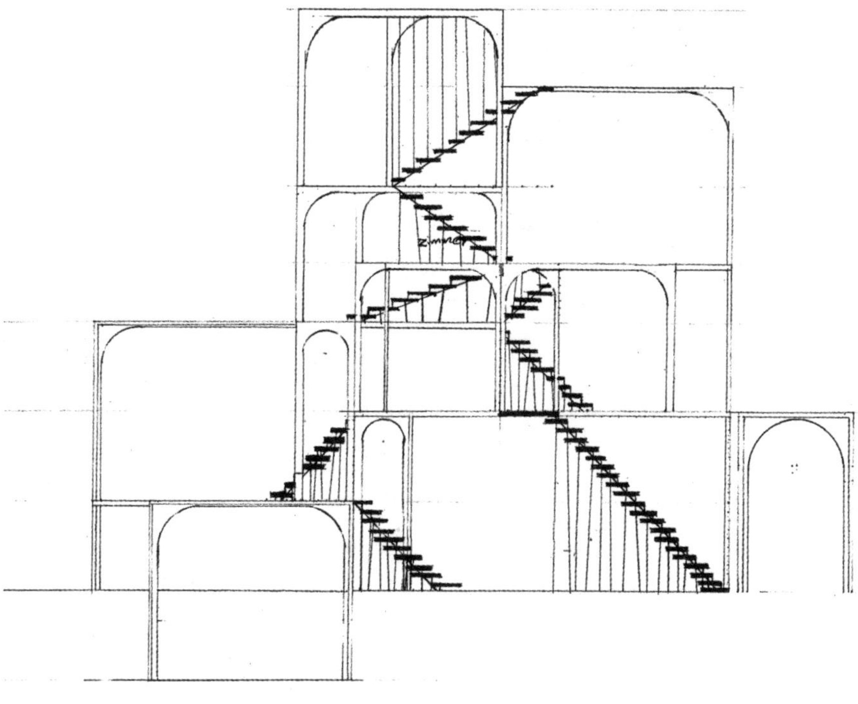
Zimmer

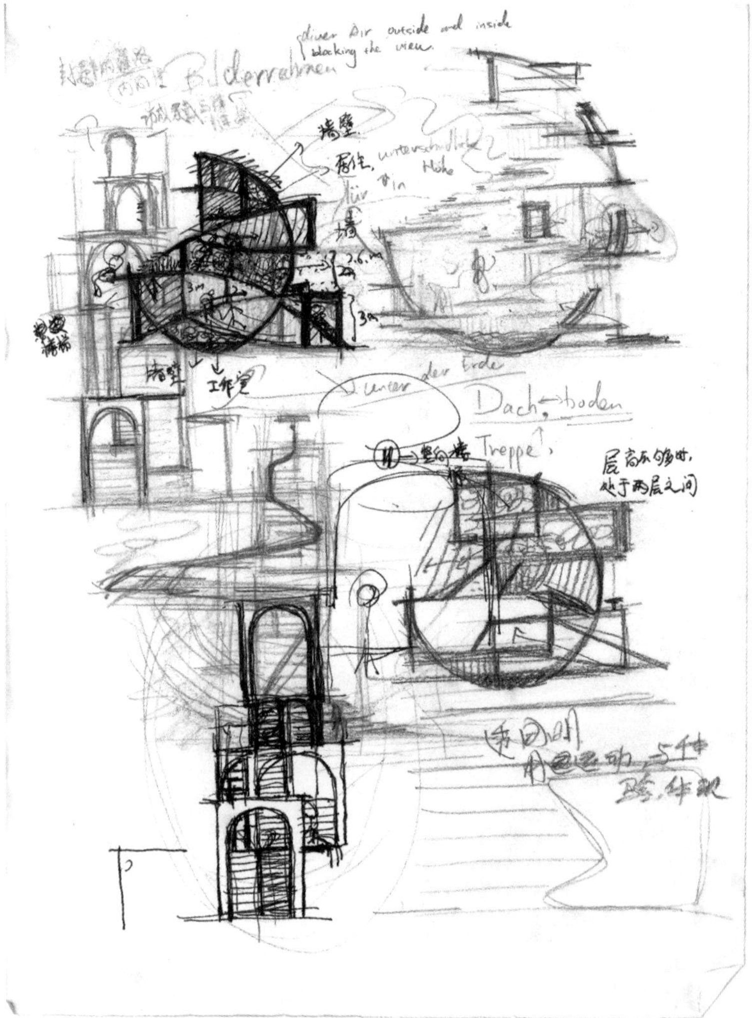
Bilderrahmen
blocking the view.
墙壁
Höhe
unter der Erde
Dach-boden
Treppe
层高不够时,
处于两层之间

A CHANCE MEETING ON A BOAT OF A BIKINI AND A COOLING TOWER

Eva Grubinger

I consciously started to think about objects as an art student in the early nineteen-nineties. It was a time when capitalism triumphed over socialism, the Internet started to take shape, and I got my first computer. A lot of my thoughts circled around questions such as: What's the difference between an object in space that I draw or that circulates on the Internet as an image? I also wanted to get to the core of the defining quality of an object: What defines its value, especially when it can be reproduced indefinitely?

Was it its materiality, the quality of execution, its surroundings; or was it the idea behind it? As an analogy I came up with a wine bottle. When we buy a bottle of wine, we might be influenced by the design of the label, the name, and the location of the vineyard it comes from, but it is widely agreed that it is not the container that is of prime importance, but the liquid inside.

Considering the making of art objects as an interrelated process between seeing, thinking, and making (or vice versa), I was also wondering whether it was possible to "outsource" parts of the process to the collector. For *Netbikini* (1995) I designed a sewing pattern for a bikini in the sizes small, medium, large, and—along with instructions—provided it for download on a website (www.evagrubinger.com/netzbikini). In the exhibition itself, visitors were able to download, print, cut out the pattern, and sew their own Netbikini in a sweatshop-like

installation involving a number of tables with sewing machines. The fabric was provided, and consisted of rolled-up transparent net curtains that I had bought at Vienna's Naschmarkt. In exchange for a photo showing the visitor wearing the unisex Netbikini (there was an instant camera available during the exhibition), the visitor received the original Netbikini label authorizing the object as an original artwork—similar to the artist's signature. This process, which a surprising number of both men and women went through, exposed their normally anonymous but now virtually naked bodies to the public gaze, paying a price of more than just money.

In the history of sculpture, the plinth—separating the work of art from everyday objects—has been a huge theme, as has been the concept of the readymade, by which artists can declare any given mass-produced item as art. In *Two Friends* (2010)—which I conceived with the sculptor Werner Feiersinger—two Swiss Army rafting boats serve as the pedestal for a piece that looks like an industrially produced I-beam. As a matter of fact it simulated a readymade, but was actually handmade. The reflection of the boats in the sculpture also creates an optical illusion, some kind of transparency. When installed on the water, it assumes an in-between presence.

The seductive quality of objects is another topic I have long contemplated in my work. *Decoy* (2011), for example, started with a fascination for fishing lures. The exhibit is comprised of sculptures made from wood and metal.

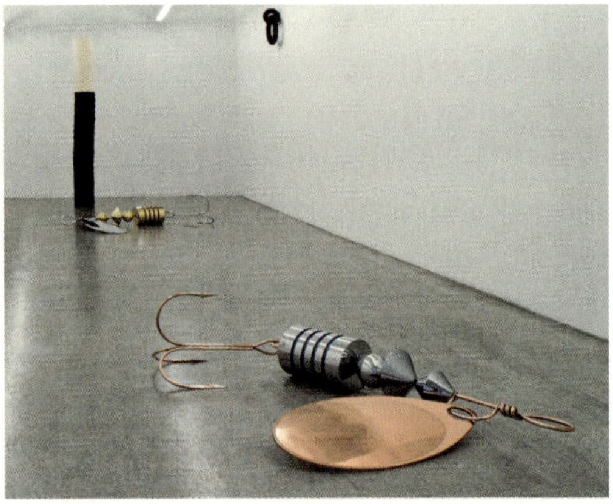

A pole and a mooring ring place the viewers underneath an imaginary water surface. Here oversized fishhooks are laid out, on which shiny cylinders, spheres, and cones of galvanized precious metals are luring. Here, by way of scaling, I want to put the objects into a new relationship to the human body. Already in their original size the fishing lures are reminiscent of jewelry. Through this leap in scale I can amplify their fetish-like character and transfer the aspect of lethal seduction from the area of fishing towards the area of human relationships.

Scaling also has another effect: When objects reach a certain size, and are located on the floor, walls, and ceiling, they become too large and heavy to manipulate. I recently used this aspect for a series of sculptures titled *Five Problems* (2016). These are based on disentanglement puzzles from China, Africa, and America, which I have been collecting over the years and which came to Europe through colonization. In their new reworked and rescaled shape the "problems" become mental ones, calisthenics for the brain. The new scale also brings to light sexual overtones, suggesting that one intractable problem could be gender relations.

Usually human relations are directed by norms and rules. As architects you know that the public sphere is quite regulated. But especially where bans become extremely obvious, they can provoke us to noncompliance, to defiant transgression, no matter how sensible the regulations might be. I wanted to dedicate a work to this phenomenon, and the commission for a public sculpture came exactly at the time when the general smoking ban was issued in Europe. *Smoking Shelter* (2010–11) is a kind of modernist smoking pavilion made of painted steel. Permanently installed in a spa park, the open smoking shelter outdoors ironizes this ban:

Here this deviant behaviour can be ritualized. The screens protect the identity of the smokers, who again can blend out this idyllic landscape while fully devoting themselves to their vice.

Blending into the landscape by looking not just at its natural dimension but also its historical and ideological ones can also inspire new shapes. A few years ago I found out about a little-known place in the Austrian Alps, the so-called Hedgehog. It served as a hideout for resistance fighters between 1943 and 45. The Hedgehog opens up the view towards the opposing mountain, in which there had been salt mines where, at the time, looted art from all over Europe was hidden. Through further research I came across the collection of Oskar Bondy, which was stolen and placed in the mine, and later saved with the help of the men hiding at the Hedgehog. The round, spiky shape of the little wooden sculpture that I was finally able to install at the hideout in 2015—seventy years after the end of the Nazi regime—is derived from a smaller, but similarly designed object that Bondy once owned, but that is missing still today.

Surfaces are another issue. Obscuring materiality can bring to light immaterial processes without the need to explain anything. I first used dark surfaces, which do not allow any conclusion on materiality, in 2003. *Dark Matter* is a group of sculptures originally conceived for an exhibition at the BALTIC Centre for Contemporary Art in Newcastle. The north of England was undergoing large socioeconomic changes at the time—moving from coal mining and shipbuilding to the services and surveillance industries. The title was borrowed from the astronomical dark matter, which forms the universe while remaining invisible itself because it is black and therefore doesn‘t reflect any light. I wanted the sculptures to emit contradictory signals. They are instantly recognizable:

an oversized headset with mirrored windows and three towers—a cooling tower, a tower block, and a control tower. But, due to their surfaces, one should not recognize what they actually are; one should not see what is in them, whether they are light or heavy, hollow or massive. Using the surfaces I tried to convey this uncertainty in regard to the visible, the material, triggered by this neoliberal conversion, and an uncanny atmosphere, which I very much sensed during that time.

Yet the exposure of materiality, its craftsmanship and tactile qualities, can convey a variety of associations. For example in *Five Problems* the use of rope, stainless steel, and fiberglass brings into play my longstanding interest in the maritime as a metaphor, particularly in regard to competition and conquest while also offering the simultaneous promise of freedom and transgression. Especially in recent years I have also been drawn towards a variety of outdoor materials, since they suggest safety, even though we put ourselves in danger with and through them.

These are a few strands of my ongoing explorations into the semiotic universe of everyday objects and materials: Taking things we might be familiar with—even to the point of no longer seeing them—and altering them so that they register anew, revealing not only themselves, but also their subtle workings on our body and mind.

ON HOUSES

Bettina Kraus, Nandini Oehlmann, Mathias Peppler

REFERENCE AND FORM

Traditionally, a room schedule or project brief taken together with other parameters like site, personal preferences, et cetera, form the starting point in the search for an architecture and the space it is intended to contain. In contrast, by critically engaging the objects, the relationship between content and form is reversed. Instead of spatially formulating the function, the preexisting space within the object is asked what it can potentially accommodate. The starting point for this dialogue is not the desire to produce a specific shape or an interest in a particular style, but rather the handmade form itself.

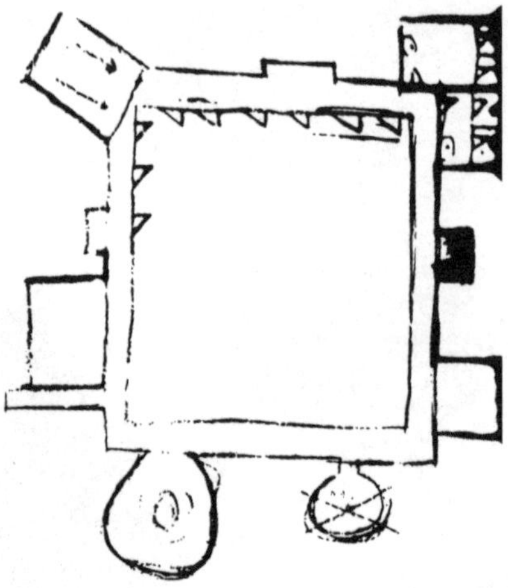

As the design process continues, and the form is charged with the parameters of function, scale, context, et cetera, the house is inevitably emancipated from the original object. Or in other words, the object automatically begins to transition from its original state of embryonic implicitness as it is observed with increased complexity. From that moment on, working with the house resembles the search for a lost ideal condition, which is simply not transferrable to reality and has to be completely redefined. As references, the objects are simultaneously extreme in their expression and in the ways they can be interpreted with respect to their material and spatial potential. Unlike using a preexisting building as a reference, the images of what can transpire within the object when it is transformed into a house still have to be generated. Questions that would otherwise arise during the design stage are already encapsulated in and radically formatted and compressed into the object so that one can focus more clearly. Material, density, circulation, et cetera, are already so tightly interwoven and extreme in their formulation that the design process can focus on more essential spatial questions. Spaces and houses emerge more from a process of omission than one of addition.

And at the same time, the objects debunk any preconceived or clichéd notions and images while their consistency in character allows for a detached working method that finds its footing solely in the piece itself. For the most part, the structures are spatially complete and just need to be understood. In this way, an eclectic working method is avoided. It becomes less a cognitive task of piecing things together and more about meaningful understanding, and as such, about the house itself as a result.

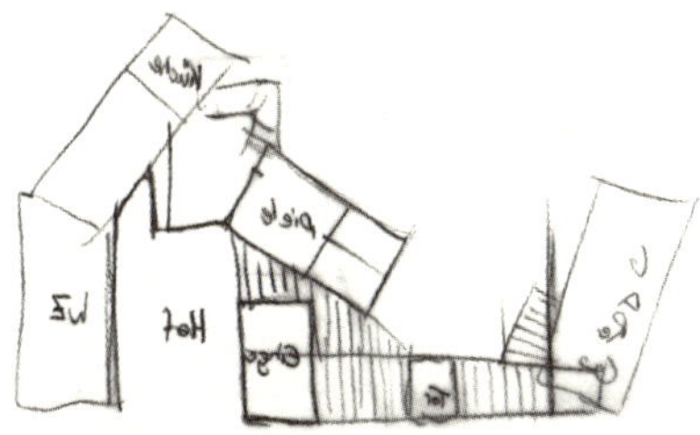

The houses thereby are handmade and arise from an authentic understanding of what was there before and what could be. They demonstrate that the relationship between space and function is hardly contingent on a general formatting, but that this can be redefined time and again. The process of inner referencing does not necessarily generate useful houses in our classic understanding of the city—in the meaning of negotiating collective space and individual interests—but leads to an architecture that is the opposite of generic space, with which we are more and more confronted in the cities where we live.

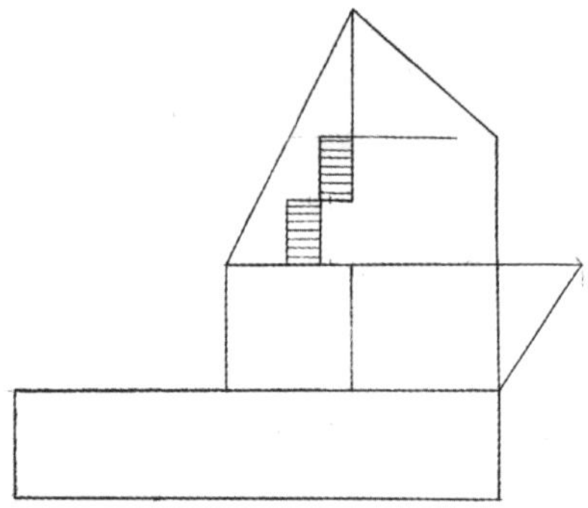

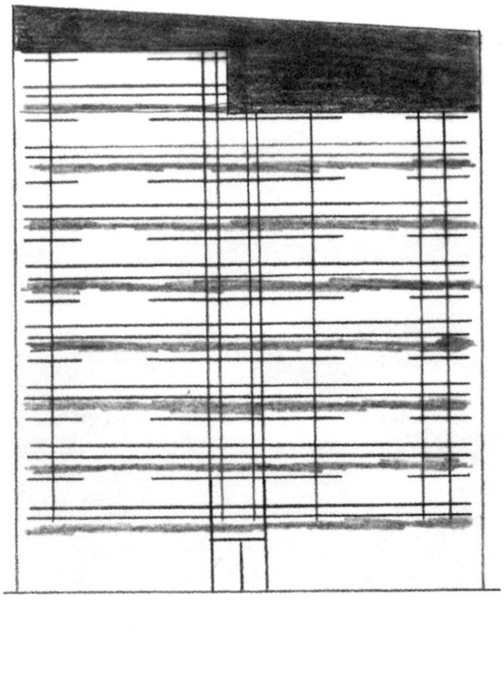

APPEARANCE AND STYLE

In teaching young students, as in our own work as architects with clients and more broadly during the developmental stages of our career, we are repeatedly confronted with a similar experience in varying contexts: The blatant obviousness of a design is readily understood while an understanding of the inherent subtleties has to be won over time. In other words, what is said loud and clear is heard by everyone, but what remains quiet and subtle is more often than not drowned out. Both instances can be found in the objects, which serve as the starting point for the design process. There are, however, hardly any applicable stylistic terms for the objects themselves: They have no context, no point of reference, and have no ambition to be anything but the forms they already are. Their appearance could be described as unplanned, as if they have no desire to convey an overarching message. They demand nothing and hence seem idle. And despite this, they retain their position as much more than mere shapes; they cannot be easily described in a sentence; and any attempt at reducing them to a core idea would remove much more than just their inexactitudes.

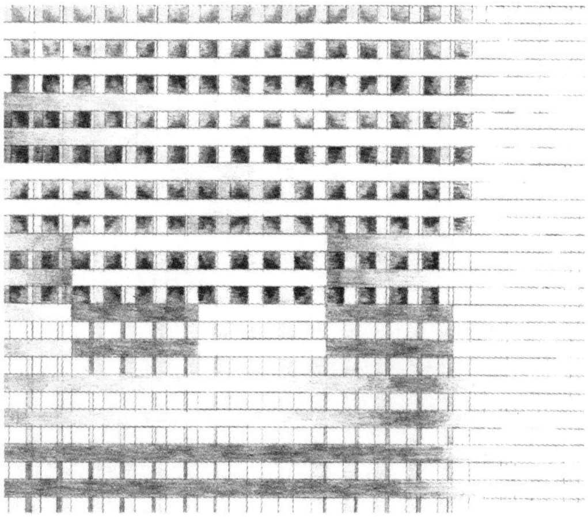

The ambivalence found in their legibility and the apparently inherent defects they possess is what transforms them into more than a mere idea, and thus into something authentic.

Converting what has transpired and its authenticity into the real world—or rather into a house—is much more difficult. By definition, context provides a fixed reference point and there are no more decisions to be made irrespective of style. One could now say that, as soon as the intention to create something is present, the moment of authentic production and nonchalance in the search for a style are lost. This is, however, not the case. This condition is just disparately more difficult to generate with a house than with an object and is only possible—

and must be acquired—through a refined understanding of the house as a form and how it can be read. The flaws of each object convert them into obstinate creations and lead to a risky balancing act in the process of becoming a house. Working with the house—or rather striking a balance between the object and the house—demonstrates quite plainly that, in both the production and our perception of space and forms, there exists a sense of what is right and wrong. It is a process of seeking out and tracking down the different

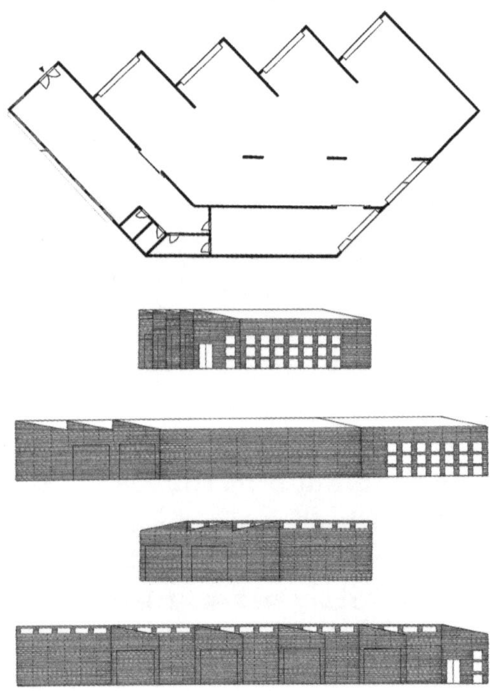

conditions of a form within a given context, whereby only through the ongoing process of refining one's observational abilities can subtlety, and with it also ambivalence, become a natural and more steadfast part of the design process.

The houses developed from working with the objects show that there is no right or wrong in regards to style and how living space is created, and that repetitive comparisons between the ideal state and reality can, in a best-case scenario, little by little, impart an understanding for the subtleties in the appearance of the form as a house. Architecture is not only created in the mind—the design process is maybe better understood as a language which at once provides a sense of what and how something should be said, and in which context this should occur. In the case of the objects and the houses, it is their forms and their figures, understood in a haptic sense, that, as immediate and sensory experiences, become the backdrop for our everyday activities.

TABLES

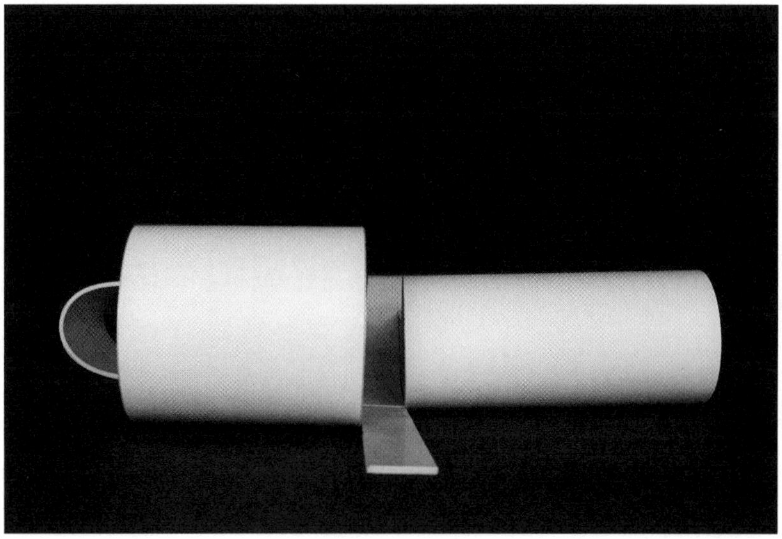

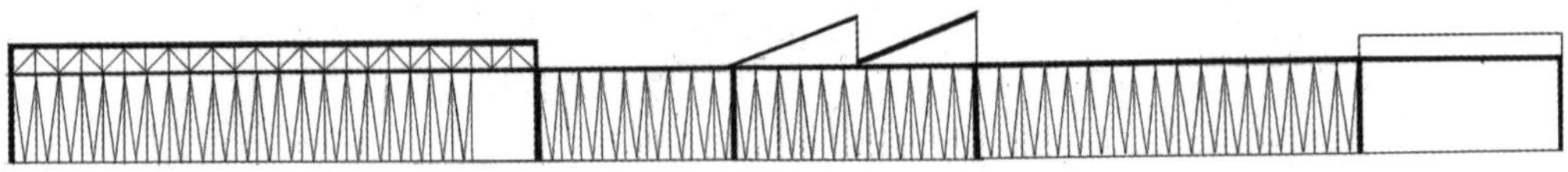

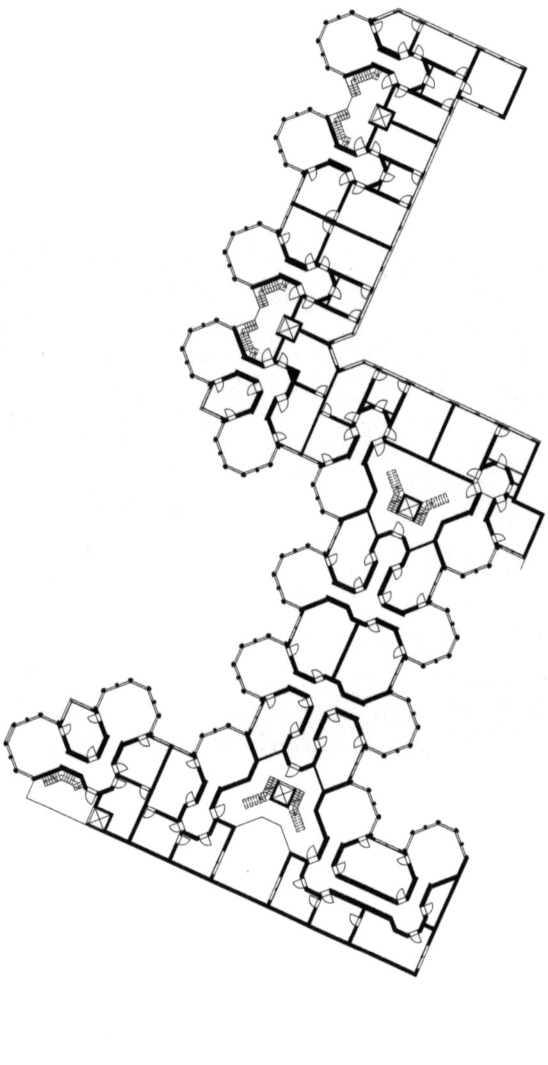

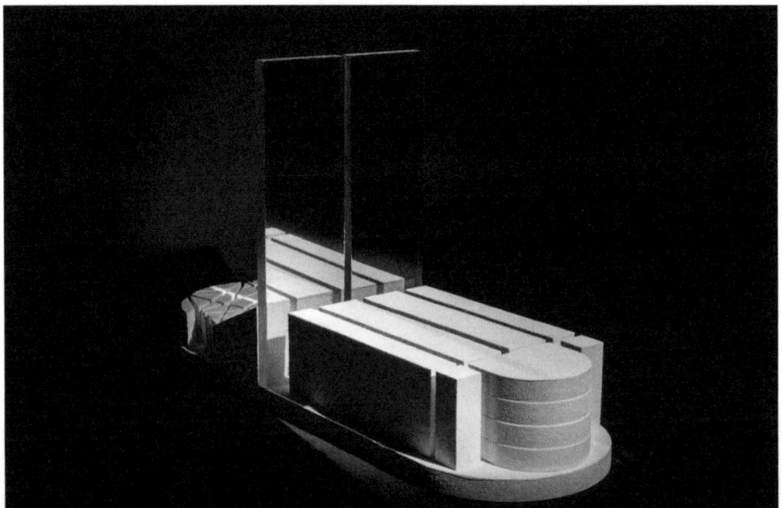

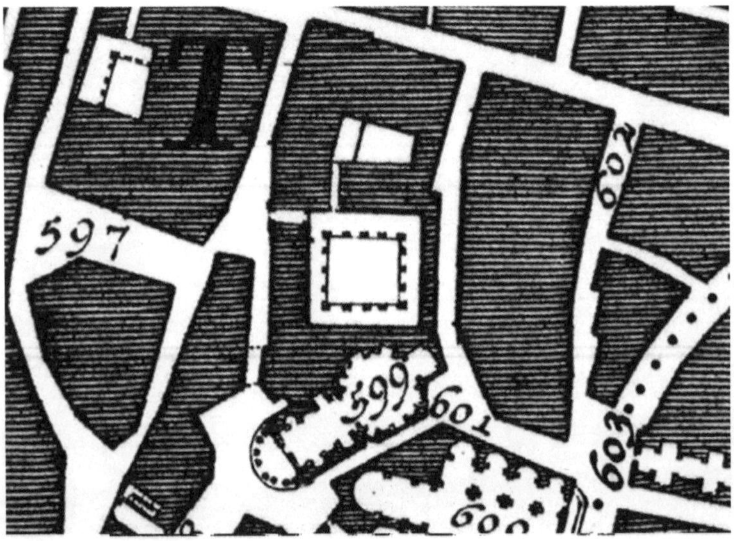
T
597
599
601
602
603

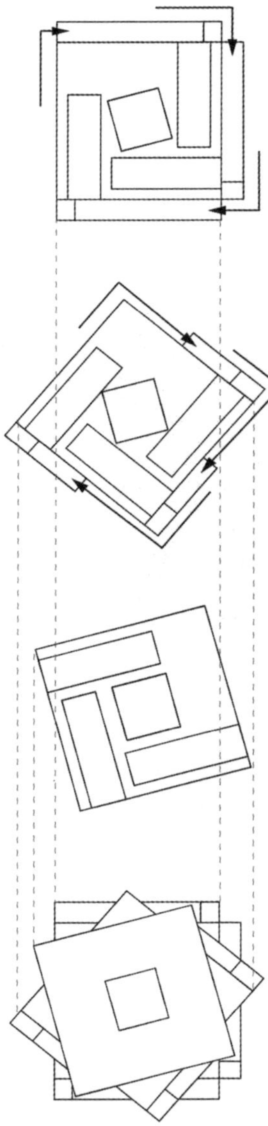

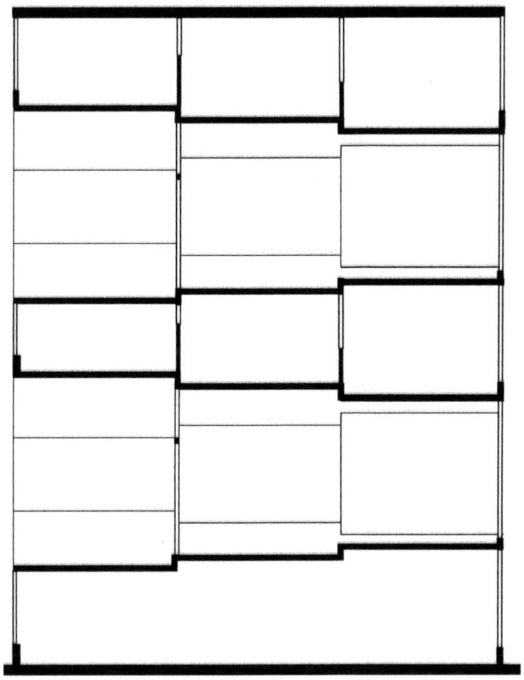

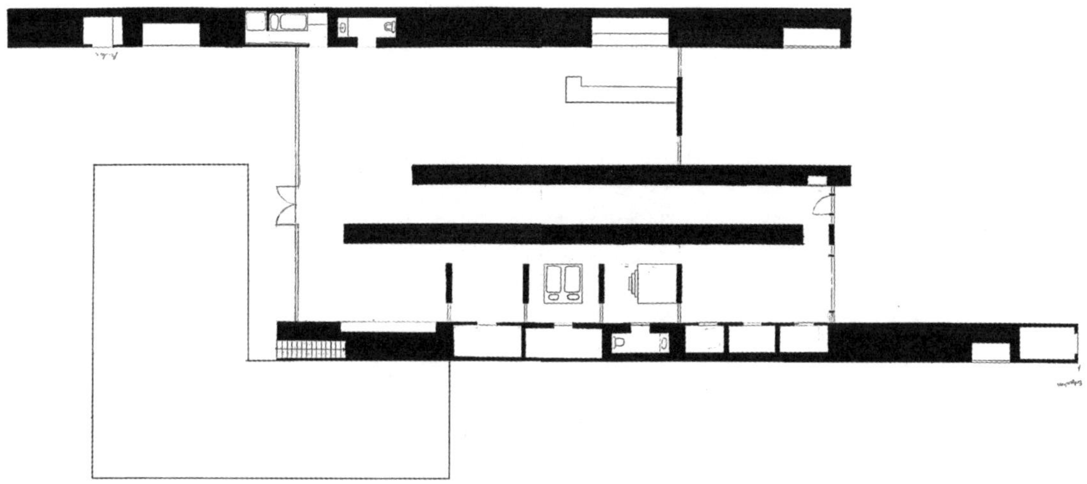

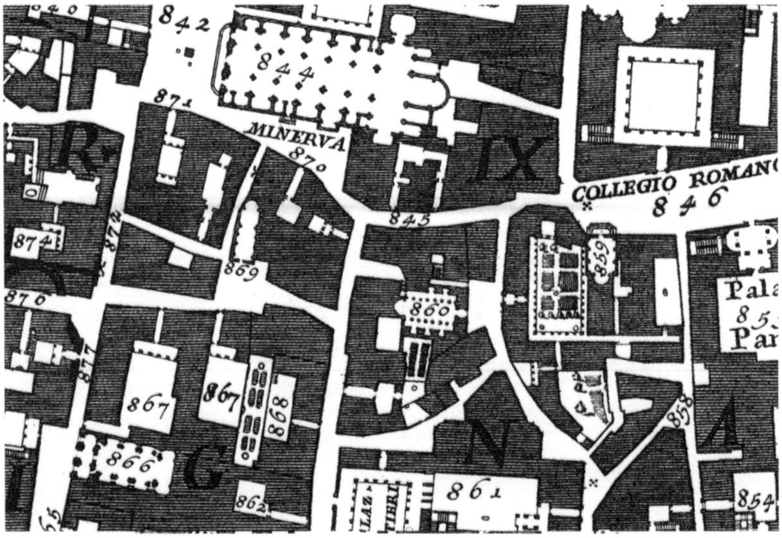
842
844
871
MINERVA
870
IX
COLLEGIO ROMAN
846
845
R
874
872
869
876
860
859
877
867
867
868
858
A
N
G
866
861
862
854

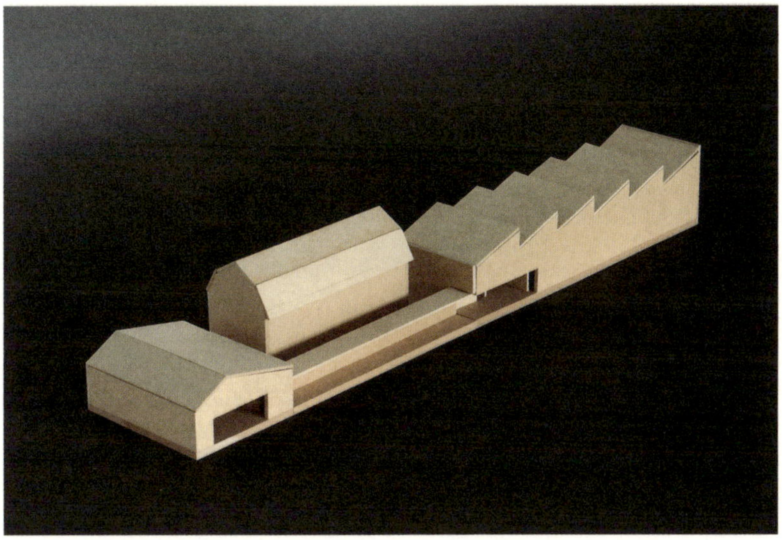

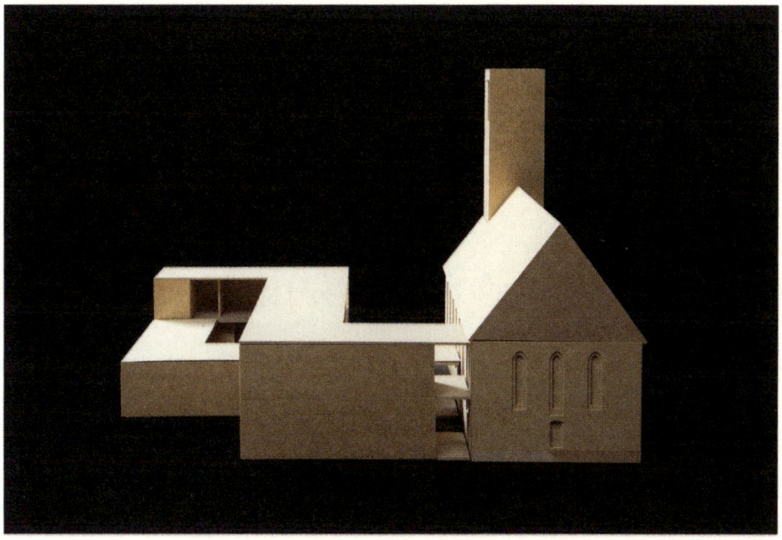

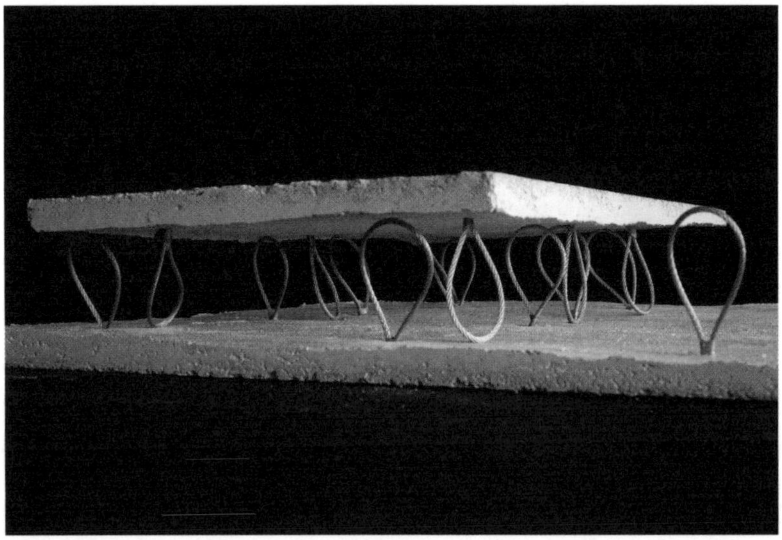

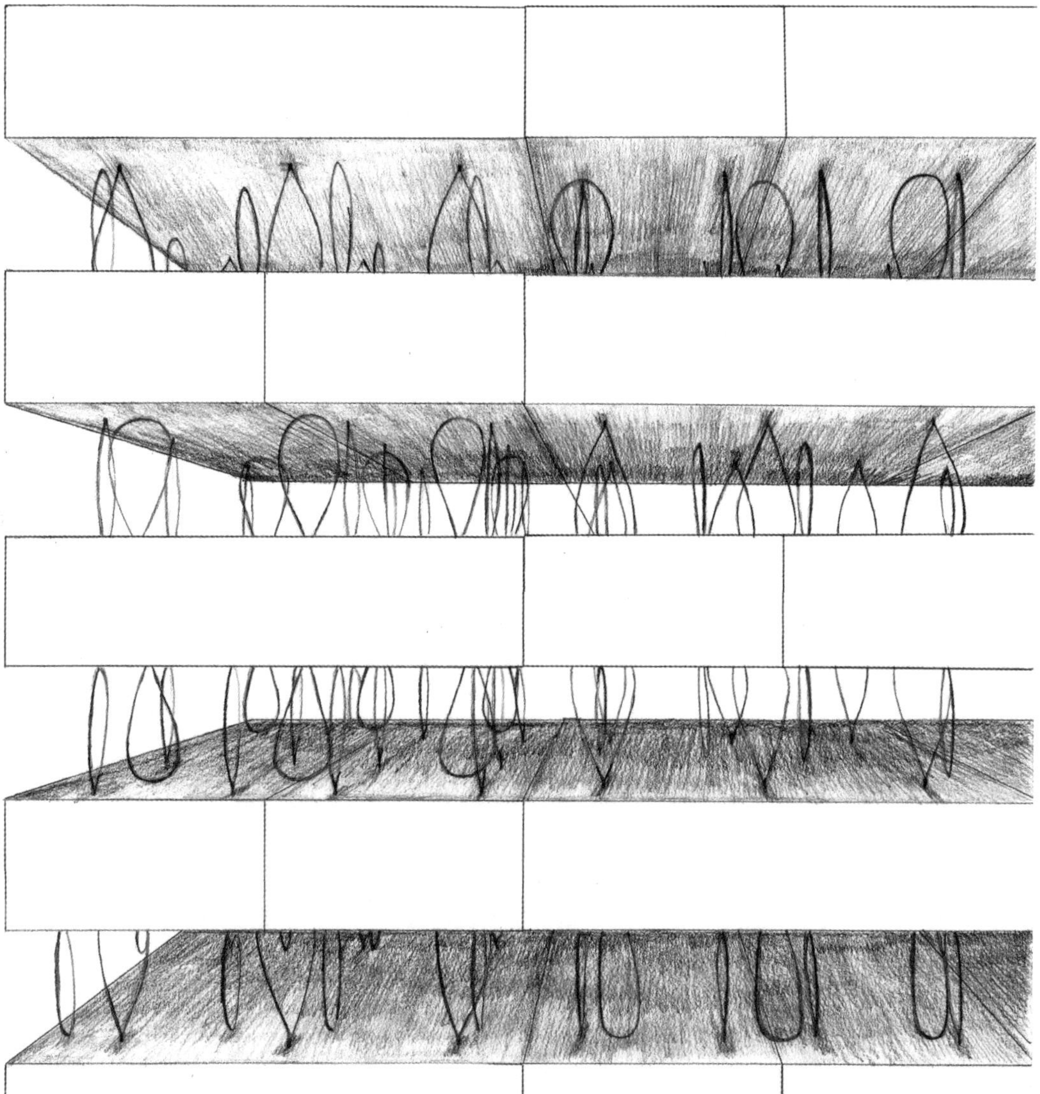

CONCRETE BODIES

Isa Melsheimer

50
50
50
50

SANCTI
HVNC FONTEM CIVES NOVI AVRELIANI
TOTO POPULO DONO DEDERUNT
1 2'90

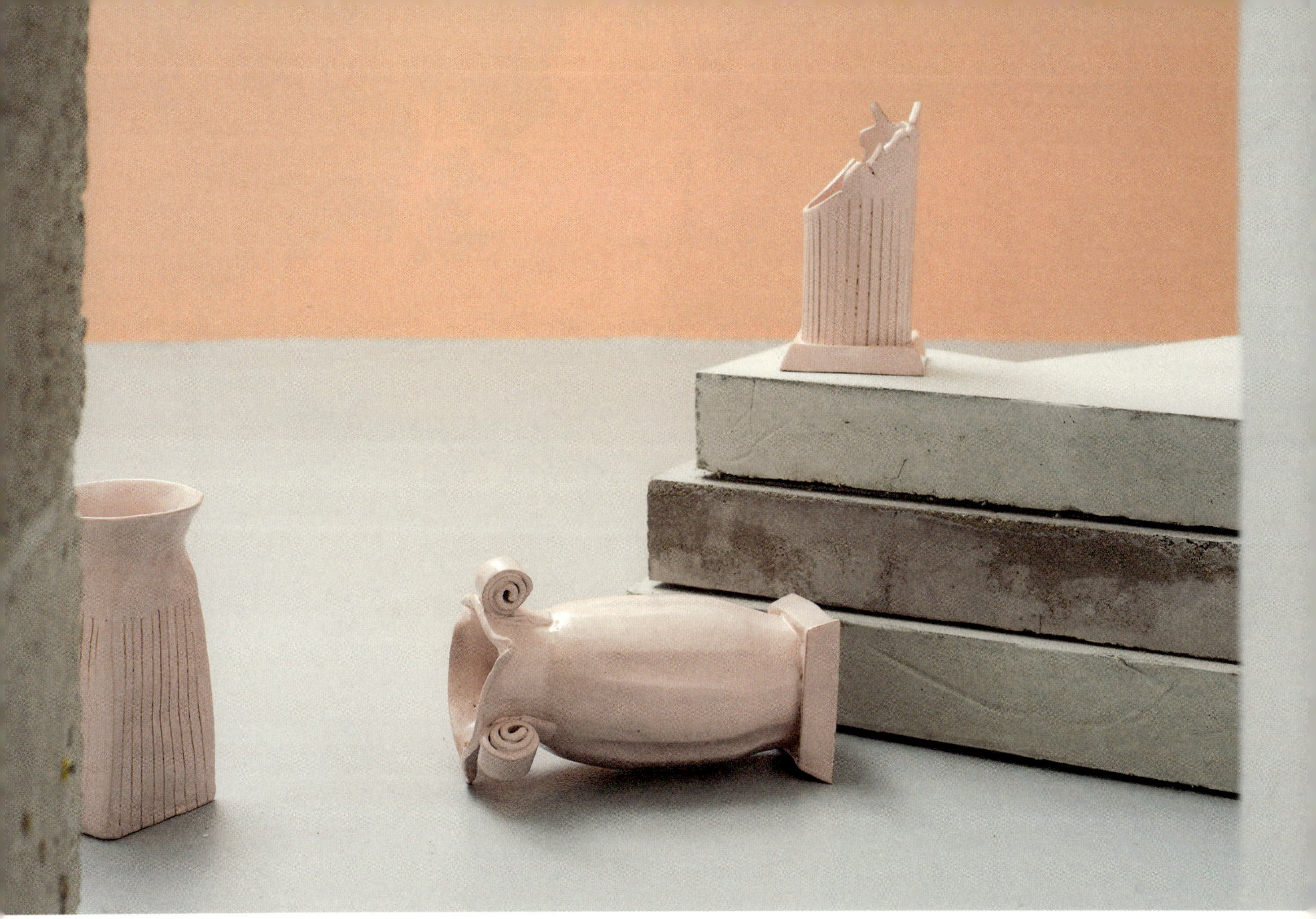

20 × 6,6
2×
20 × 15
20 × 18,6
50 × 20
35 × 15
51,6 × 15

AUTHORS

BETTINA KRAUS

Bettina Kraus, born in 1970, studied architecture at the Swiss Federal Institute of Technology Zurich, the Berlin University of the Arts, and the University of Stuttgart, from which she received her diploma in 1996. From 1997 to 2012 she worked with Wiel Arets Architects, initially in Maastricht. She became a partner in 2000 and was in charge of setting up the office in Amsterdam. Her main tasks revolved around leading and overseeing the design of numerous prizewinning projects and competitions. In 2013, she moved back to Germany to found the architectural practice Thomas Baecker Bettina Kraus in Berlin.

Her projects span a wide range of functions and scales, from towers to teapots, from affordable housing to custom-made cultural spaces. Highly complex spatial programs illustrate an ongoing interest in typological modifications. Due to connections with product and furniture design she is familiar with the conditions and parameters of industrial production. Bettina Kraus was an assistant professor at the Berlin University of Arts between 2004 and 2010. After that, she headed the design program at the Berlin Studio of Northeastern University between 2011 and 2014. Currently she is leading the chair of Architectural Design and Building in Context at Brandenburg University of Technology Cottbus.

MICHAEL BEUTLER

Michael Beutler, born in 1976, is a sculptor and installations artist. He studied art at the Städelschule in Frankfurt am Main from 1997 to 2003 and at the Glasgow School of Art from 2000 to 2001. Making tools to make his installations became the core principle of his approach during this time. He uses industrially manufactured materials such as paper, metal, wood, or plastic, shaping them with his own invented machines into large-scale building elements and architectural sculptures that refer to their particular immediate context and its distinctive characteristics.

Michael Beutler's work has been shown in a range of solo exhibitions across Europe and group exhibitions from Columbia to Japan. He also has permanent installations, including *Polder Peil*, a family of staggered concrete ball sculptures that measures the landscape in Zeeland, Holland; and the handmade seventeen-meter-high *Aluminium Pagoda* that reflects the office architecture of the Lufthansa Aviation Center at the Frankfurter Airport. His installation *Shipyard* is part of the 57th Venice Biennale. "Moby Dick," his biggest show so far, took over the historic hall of Berlin's Hamburger Bahnhof in 2015. Since 2016 he has taught as guest professor at the Muthesius University of Fine Arts and Design.

EVA GRUBINGER

While Eva Grubinger, born in 1970, began her art career with pioneering works that reflected and commented on the Internet's early development, since the mid-1990s she has worked primarily in sculpture and installation. These phases are connected: Her latter-day focus on materiality and space, not least social space and its subliminal effects, might be seen as a reaction to the online world's immateriality. While focusing on recognizable objects, her scope is wide, drawing on seafaring, history, architecture, the theatre of politics, and recent art history—particularly minimalism and conceptualism—and spans formats and materials. Subjects we might be familiar with, to the point of not "seeing" them, are transformed in scale, context, material, and surface, so that the familiar reveals both itself and its subtle, often politicized workings on body and mind.

In the 1990s and 2000s, Eva Grubinger had numerous international residencies and held professorships at the University of Art and Design Linz and the Düsseldorf Art Academy. Her works have been widely shown internationally: in solo exhibitions at the Kiasma Museum, Helsinki; Berlinische Galerie, Berlin; Schirn Kunsthalle, Frankfurt; Museum Belvedere, Vienna; and the ICA, London, among others; and in many group exhibitions at venues such as the Deichtorhallen, Hamburg; the Taipei Fine Art Museum; the Krannert Art Museum in Champaign, Illinois; the Marrakech Biennale; and the Witte de With Center, Rotterdam.

ALICJA KWADE

Alicja Kwade, born in 1979, received a degree in sculpture from the Berlin University of the Arts in 2005. Her work investigates and questions the structures of our reality and society and reflects on the perception of time in our everyday life. Her diverse practice is based around concepts of space, time, science, and philosophy, and takes shape in sculptural objects, video, and even photography. Common objects such as bikes, bottles, clocks, and tables, or low-value materials such as glass, wood, coal, and stone are restructured through elaborate, alchemical operations. Through these physical transformations she processes new meaning, shifts value, and spans illusions.

Alicja Kwade's exhibitions include solo shows at the Whitechapel Gallery, London; Kunsthalle Schirn, Frankfurt am Main; and Hamburger Bahnhof, Berlin. Her work has been seen in many group exhibitions, including at the Bass Museum of Art, Miami Beach; Kunsthalle Wien, Vienna; Museum of Contemporary Art Detroit; Galerie des Galeries Lafayette, Paris; and the Museum of Contemporary Art, Tokyo. The Public Art Fund commissioned the installation *Against the Run*, placed in New York's Central Park. She is taking part in the third Kochi-Muziris Biennale, the 57th Venice Biennale, and the first ARoS Triennial in Aarhus.

ISA MELSHEIMER

Berlin-based artist Isa Melsheimer, born in 1968, studied at the Berlin University of the Arts between 1991 and 1997. She deals with urban spaces and the conditions surrounding their design and change. She is as interested in the vocabulary of forms of modern architecture as in urban design scenarios and the dynamics of their corresponding social tensions. Isa Melsheimer develops complex spatial installations with surprising leaps in scale, changing vantage points, and material contrasts in reaction to the specific sites of her exhibitions. In addition to concrete, glass, or ceramic sculptures, her experimental model-like compositions also include embroidered curtains, arrangements of collected objects, or live plant ensembles. The sculptural works are accompanied by gouache paintings, whose imagery is permeated by overlapping citations from the fields of art, architecture, design, and pop culture.

Isa Melsheimer's work has been shown in solo exhibitions at art3, Valence; Quartz Studio, Turin; Ernst Barlach Haus, Hamburg; Santa Monica Museum of Art, Los Angeles; and Carré d'Art, Nimes. She also took part in many group shows, including at Espace Louis Vuitton, Paris; Domaine Du Muy, Le Muy; Museum Morsbroich, Leverkusen; and Kunsthalle Wien, Vienna. Since 2016 she has been guest professor for experimental drawing at the Braunschweig University of Art.

NANDINI OEHLMANN

Nandini Oehlmann, born in Berlin in 1985, graduated in architecture in 2013 after studying at the Berlin University of the Arts and the Technical University of Istanbul. She has been academic assistant at the chair of Architectural Design and Building in Context at the Brandenburg University of Technology Cottbus since 2014 and has been working in architectural practice. Her focus lies on private housing and made-to-measure interiors. She has been a doctoral candidate at the Berlin University of the Arts since 2017, researching embodied knowledge in architectural design.

MATHIAS PEPPLER

Mathias Peppler, born 1979 in Heidelberg, studied architecture at the Karlsruher Institute of Technology and the University of East London, graduating in 2008. After working for different architecture offices in Basel and Berlin he became academic assistant at the chair of Architectural Design and Building in Context at the Brandenburg University of Technology Cottbus in 2011. He has been running his own office, MATA Architeken, in Berlin since 2012. Together with his partner Markus Tauber, their emphasis lies in building conversions.

IMAGE CREDITS

p.8, 9: *1979 leere Liter bis zum Anfang*, 2010, 2240 kg empty champagne glass bottles with labels, pulverized, h 93 cm, Ø 267 cm, Installation view, Hamburger Kunstverein, Alicja Kwade, Images © Raimund Zakowski
p.10: *Lampe*, 2016, ground lamp, epoxy resin, glass, brass, 155 x 40 x 40 cm, Alicja Kwade, Image © Roman März
p.11: Image © Alicja Kwade
p.12: *Lampe (Kaiser Idell rot)*, 2015, iron 2079 g, plastic 84.4 g, brass 30.2 g, copper 24.3 g, glass 19.4 g, aluminium 13.6 g, ceramic 10.7 g, cotton 9.1 g, outer varnish 6.2 g, paper 3.8 g, inner varnish 2.8 g, Wolfram 0.01 g, 14 jars, vitrine, 132 x 172 x 33 cm, Alicja Kwade, Image © Roman März
p.13: *Parallelwelt 2*, 2008, ten Kaiser-Idell lamps, ten mirrors 98 x 56 x 300 cm, Alicja Kwade, Image © Roman März
p.14, 15: *Ein Tisch ist ein Bild*, 2017, wood, mirror, 107 x 85 x 85 cm, Alicja Kwade, Images © Roman März
p.16-48: *On Objects,* Images © BTU Cottbus
p.30: The New Plan of Rome, Detail, Giambattista Nolli, 1748
p.50-57: Images © Michael Beutler
p.56, 57 top: Spike Images © Stuart Whipps
p.58-88: *On Making*, Images © BTU Cottbus
p.76: The New Plan of Rome, Detail, Giambattista Nolli, 1748
p.90: *Netbikini*, 1995, Detail, C-Print, 70 x 100 cm, Eva Grubinger © VG Bildkunst, Bonn
p.91: *Two Friends*, 2010, in collaboration with Werner Feiersinger, rafting boats, stainless steel, concrete, Melk-Danube, Eva Grubinger © VG Bildkunst, Bonn
p.92, 93: *Decoy*, 2011, Installation view and Detail, Kerstin Engholm Gallery, Vienna, Eva Grubinger © VG Bildkunst, Bonn
p.94: *Hedgehog*, 2014-15, Installation view, Igel, Salzkammergut, Eva Grubinger © VG Bildkunst, Bonn
p.95: *Smoking Shelter*, 2010-11, Installation view and Detail, Kunstwegen, Bad Bentheim, Eva Grubinger © VG Bildkunst, Bonn
p.96 left: *Dark Matter*, Installation view, Berlinische Galerie, Berlin, 2003, plywood, paint, sound, 390 x 450 x 410 cm, Detail, Eva Grubinger © VG Bildkunst, Bonn
p.96, 97: *Five Problems*, 2016, Installation view, Bloomberg Space, London, Eva Grubinger © VG Bildkunst, Bonn

p.98-128: *On Houses*,
Images © BTU Cottbus
p.114, 112: The New Plan of Rome, Detail, Giambattista Nolli, 1748
p.130: Casa Mastroianni, architect: Enzo Venturelli with Umberto Mastroianni,
Image © Isa Melsheimer
p.131: *Casa Mastroianni*, 2015 fiberglass, reinforced concrete, ceramic, Isa Melsheimer,
Image © Beppe Giardino
p.132: Beistegui Penthouse, architect: Le Corbusier,
Image © Isa Melsheimer
p.133: *Dachgarten*, 2010 concrete, metal, cypress, 90 x 54 x 40.5 cm, Isa Melsheimer,
Image © François Doury
p.134: Piazza d'Italia, New Orleans, 1979, architect: Charles Moore,
Image © Isa Melsheimer
p.135: *Tea and Coffee Piazza d'Italia in Post-Katrina Times*, 2013, reinforced concrete, ceramic, 45 x 205 x 70 cm, Isa Melsheimer,
Image © François Doury
p.136: Runcorn, architect: Charles Stirling, Image © Isa Melsheimer
p.137: *Possibility Of A Ruin IX*, 2016, reinforced concrete, ceramic, plinth three parts 50.5 x 50 x 50 cm, 27 x 15 x 10 cm, 100 x 50 x 50, Isa Melsheimer,
Image © Andrea Rossetti

STUDENTS 2014-2017

Qosay Amer, Cecil Ari, Annika Bange, Constantin Beiküfner, Lydia Beyers, Marius Birnbreier, Anna Böhm, Lukas Breuning, Gerburg Brilling, Ali Dogan, Chantal Drescher, Lisa Eberhard, Adrian Ebert, Halina Eirich, Jean Falkenberg, Jonas Flache, Franziska Fohler, Sara Foustok, Jasper Franke, Nina Fritsche, Khalil Funke, Rebecca Galley, Sophia Gansauge, Vithujan Gengatharan, Pascal Gorkiewicz, Branko Gudlin, Pauline Gust, Leana Hahn, Janluka Haselwander, Vivienne Heiden, Eric Heinze, Juliane Henkel, Rafael Herzberger, Nicklas Heseltine, Dennis Hildebrandt, Maximilan Hoffmann, Julia Ihl, Marcel Iliades, Niko Iliades, Görkem Kablan, Caroline Kämmerer, Jannik Kastrup, Adrianna Klaja, Lisa Kutsche, Blerta Lahu, Yunshan Li, Henrik Lück, Nina Marquardt, Moritz Mayer, Katharina Mientz, Izabella Milto, Leon Morscher, Mounira Moussalli, Michael Nguyen, Joanna Olszowy, Aleksandra Oracz, Thomas Pawelczyk, Xinyao Peng, Miryana Petrova, Lara Philipp, Victoria Radicke, Karl Raucamp, Adrianna Rauer, Daniel Rinza, Niklas Röhnert, Alina Schanz,

Aaron Schedler, Stephanie Scheu, Jessica Schley, Christopher Schwenke, Alexej Schwindt, Burhan Sezdi, Maximilian Springer, Hanna Strahl, Viktoria Tissen, Ayse Tunali, Nick Ulrich, Nadine Walz, Patrick Warman, Leon Weiße, Vincent Wildhirt, Yannick Wojtowicz, Lucas Zeibe, Michal Zimolag

Thanks to the students for their approval to publish their work; to Irina Hoppe, Paul Kölle, and Kay Michalczack for photographing the models; to our student assistants Boris Giebichenstein, Leana Hahn, Hanna Heber, Rafael Herzberger, Dennis Hildebrand, Ferdinand List, Janosch Ottenschläger, and our secretary Mandy Metag; Thomas Baecker, Roger Bundschuh, Ute Frank, Ole Hallier, Martin Herbert, Gwendolyn Kerschbaumer, and Bruno Röver for their kind support.

Supported by: Brandenburgische Technische Universität Cottbus-Senftenberg

Authors: Bettina Kraus, Michael Beutler, Eva Grubinger, Alicja Kwade, Isa Melsheimer, Nandini Oehlmann, Mathias Peppler

Editor: Niklas Fanelsa
Design: Something Fantastic
Art Department, Leonard Streich
Translation: Eric Zapel
Proofreading: Christen Jamar

Printed in the EU

Bibliographic information published by the Deutsche Nationalbibliothek. The Deutsche Nationalbibliothek lists this publication in the Deutsche Nationalbibliografie; detailed bibliographic data are available on the Internet at http://dnb.d-nb.de.

jovis Verlag GmbH
Kurfürstenstraße 15/16
10785 Berlin
www.jovis.de

jovis books are available worldwide in select bookstores. Please contact your nearest bookseller or visit www.jovis.de for information concerning your local distribution.

ISBN 978-3-86859-463-8